POWER LUNCHING

Turnbull & Willoughby

POWER LUNCHING

HOW YOU CAN PROFIT FROM MORE

EFFECTIVE BUSINESS LUNCH STRATEGY

E. Melvin Pinsel
Ligita Dienhart

ISBN: 0-943084-07-5

Library of Congress Catalog Card Number   83-51693

First printing January 1984

Manufactured in the United States of America

Published by Turnbull & Willoughby Publishers, Inc., Willoughby Towers, 8 South Michigan, Chicago, IL 60603.

10 9 8 7 6 5 4 3 2 1

Cover design by Zimnicki Studios
Illustrations by Chris Roth

DEDICATION

An idea is nothing until it is put to work.

A chance meeting (in a restaurant of course) led to the renewal of an old friendship that stimulated the authors to work on the idea for "Power Lunching."

Particular thanks are offered by co-author E. Melvin Pinsel to Howard Grafman for his encouragement, ideas, and support for this project. Special thanks are given by co-author Ligita Dienhart to Murrey S. who did not live to see the results of his inspiration and belief in my abilities.

In the main, our book is dedicated to its readers. For only when the readers gain from its content, do the authors profit from their idea put to work.

Table of Contents

Chapter One
Business Lunch or Power Lunch?
Time to Take Control   11

Chapter Two
Who to Invite and How
The 3-Way, the 4-Way and Inviting the Boss   19

Chapter Three
Planning the Strategy
Foreplay and Making Your Move   31

Chapter Four
The Woman Invites
How to Have Him Eating Out of Your Hand   43

Chapter Five
Choosing the Restaurant
Making the Power Choice   55

Chapter Six
Your Assistants: The Restaurant Staff
Jacques, Pierre,,,and Jose   69

Chapter Seven
Choosing the Power Seat
Jockeying for Position   81

Chapter Eight
Liquor and the Power Lunch
"Straight up and Hold the Umbrella"   93

Chapter Nine
The Menu and the Meal
You Are What You Order   105

Chapter Ten
Getting Down to Business
Beware the Dog and Pony   119

Chapter Eleven
The Finale: The Check and the Tip
The End of a Beautiful Relationship   129

Chapter Twelve
Sex and the Power Lunch
Dining Thigh to Thigh   137

Chapter Thirteen
Power After Hours
Lunch vs Dinner Meetings   149

Chapter Fourteen
Power Lunches Within Your Company
How to Power Lunch Your Boss   159

Chapter Fifteen
Common Errors, Mistakes and Screw-ups
Power Disasters: The Long and Short of it   177

Chapter Sixteen
The Great American Power Lunch Test
Update and Scorecard   189

Chapter Seventeen
Where Power Lunchers Meet
A Sampler Coast to Coast   197

Power or Wimp?
Answers to the Great American Power Lunch Test   217

Chapter One

Business Lunch or Power Lunch?

Time to Take Control

1

"One of the all-time great power lunches occurred at the Occidental Restaurant in Washington during the Cuban missile crisis. The Soviet ambassador to the United States had called John Scali, foreign correspondent for ABC, and said he wanted to have lunch with him.

"At the restaurant, the ambassador said, 'John, I've asked you here in order to tell you Mr. Krushchev wants a way out of this thing.' And it was Scali, after that lunch, who went to President Kennedy . . .

"Imagine, here are these two superpowers, eyeball to eyeball in this international drama, and as a result of that lunch, there was a way out. It shows you how important lunches can really be.

"Later, they put a plaque next to that table in the Occidental Restaurant: 'Here sat John Scali.'"

> Tom Roeser
> Lobbyist,
> Washington, D.C.

Not all power lunches involve politics or individuals as important on the world scene as these two. As we think back in time, there have been meetings between kings and princes, gypsy tribal leaders, carpetbaggers and Indians, attorneys and politicians, statesmen and dictators, lords and commoners, merchants and buyers. Surely, we can envision food and drink being served. Aha . . . a business lunch!

But we'll never know if any of these meetings qualified as *power* lunches or dinners. Whether the participants took the time in advance to analyze their "opponent," strategically plan their moves and, most important, maneuver to keep control or power, is debatable. but be assured that today, perhaps as in times past, there are businessmen and women who realize it's inefficient to have a mere haphazard business encounter over a meal.

They are the kind of people who maximize their impact, who insist on achieving and maintaining control and influence, who shrewdly seek the advantage in every circumstance, who take assertive roles in shaping the course of events. They are the ones who set standards for success. They understand that no part of their business strategy can be slighted, that planning always pays off, that results don't just *happen*, they must be wrung out of opportunities.

These are the Power Lunchers.

What's the difference between an ordinary business lunch and a power lunch? As you'll see, it's like the difference between a flashlight and a laser. Both emit beame of light, but the flashlight does little more than illuminate the surface of things. The laser is more focused, more intense — more powerful.

Here's a quick definition of power lunching to keep in mind: It's the *studied practice of using control of a business meeting at lunch to gain your business objectives.*

The business lunch itself grew out of a real need. No, it's not just an excuse to tune-out for a few hours at midday, feed yourself and have a couple drinks with business associates. Not that there's anything wrong with that, as long as your motives are merely to satisfy your appetite and socialize with your customers, prospects or peers.

There is, though, something missing for the success-oriented businessman. In addition to the desire to eat and talk, there's the *quest for gain*. Whether you define gain as money, status or influence, whether you see it as material or abstract, we meet to discuss business essentially for gain. Nothing wrong with that, either.

In the business world, meetings are an omnipresent phenomenon. Secretary on phone: "Sorry, Mr. Smith, but Mr. Jones is in a *meeting*. May I have him return your call?" "Bill, I'd like to meet your new man, but I'm in *meetings* all day tomorrow." "Can't stop for coffee this morning, Tom, I've got a *meeting* at 9:30." Nobody, it seems, simply talks to another person these days. Things must be discussed in *meetings*.

Here's an interesting sidelight: Webster's New World Dictionary says the word "discuss" has an old colloquial meaning: "To eat or drink (something) with enjoyment." Hmmmmmm. An appropriate link between merely talking about matters in a meeting and the time-honored practice of hashing them out over lunch.

Most meetings can be looked at as an exchange between buyers and sellers. Remember, selling something encompasses more than merely providing a product or service for money or barter. You may have an idea on reducing the incidence of teenage suicide or building a non-profit community center. You've got to *sell* your ideas.

Where are the majority of meetings held? In offices, of course, and that presents a constant problem: interruptions. You've seen it happen a thousand times. Big-time executive is behind his imposing desk, a visitor — the "seller" — sits across from him in the guest chair.

"And the key to this whole thing," says the visitor, "the thing that will really make this deal fly, is ——"

Buzzzzzz. "Hold on, Charlie. I've got to take this call . . . just be a minute." Same voice five minutes later, to phone: "Look, John, I'll get back to you on that. I'm in a *meeting*. Yea, g'bye." To the guest: "Now, what were we talking about?"

Guest: 'Uh, let's see. I forgot where I was . . ."

The problem is that the person doing the selling didn't have the *advantage*. The meeting didn't transpire as he had planned because he didn't have *control*. He didn't get results because he lacked *power* — he played his game in the buyer's arena.

He loses.

GET CONTROL

To gain influence over the situation, you've got to change the meeting site to a location where *you've* got control, where *your* power is accentuated, where the environment will work to *your* advantage. And let's face it: From your youngest years, you can remember family and friends gathered around a meal, talking, eating, smiling, laughing. They were enjoying themselves. Food and drink allow people an opportunity for a *meeting*, whether purely for enjoyment, as in a social setting, or with the added stimulus of business, as in a power lunch. Business today may be hard, cold, bottom-line. Yet business is also made up of ordinary people who may be dedicated to their company's profits, but who still enjoy the pleasure of getting together with others in a warmer, more congenial atmosphere than their office.

Think about this, though: Instead of just inviting a business prospect or client to lunch, what if you brought to bear all your knowledge and experience in planning? You wouldn't hold an important business meeting or presentation in your office without orchestrating it, would you? A power lunch is a meeting, too — a meeting with a meal. Why not use those same organizational techniques to stack the cards in your favor? If you understand some basic psychological and strategic tactics, you can turn a mundane business lunch into a power lunch — and come out a winner.

What do you gain if you're skillful enough to pull off a power lunch? You gain control. You gain power. You increase your opportunity to succeed.

Think about the advantages. How long does a lunch take — one and a half or two hours? You're already ahead in the game. Most office meetings won't give you nearly that much time, yet you've managed to reserve a large chunk of the "buyer's" valuable day — all to yourself.

What's more, you'll be in a much more advantageous proximity to your prospect or client. In an office, there's usually a desk separating you from him — a desk that gives him not-so-subtle power advantage. In a restaurant, you're much closer to him. The physical barriers have been broken down. More than that, the social conversation, the food and the drinks will help dissolve personal barriers between you. Since you choose the restaurant, your guest may ask for suggestions about what's best to eat there. He's relying on you for advice; you've grown closer. And since you've primed the maitre d' beforehand, all the action of the restaurant staff is centered on you. That enhances your power.

Remember, at a restaurant your guest can't be the same tough, mean son-of-a-bitch he is in his office. When he's savoring tender veal or delicious trout, or when he's ducking his calorie count and indulging in a Napoleon, he's more vulnerable to your pitch.

At a power lunch, *you have control.*

1. Your guest's phone won't ring.

2. Uninvited people won't pop in to interrupt.

3. Your guest won't be called away for another meeting.

You call all the shots.

You suggest cocktails.

You request menus.

You suggest specialties of the house.

You provide the subject of the conversation to please and draw out your guest.

You are catered to by the restaurant staff.

You choose the time to introduce the *business reason* for the meeting.

You pay the bill.

You win the psychological battle of "who's on top" much in the same manner that speakers on raised podiums enjoy an advantage over audience members who sit on a lower level, looking up.

It's *your* show. The spotlight is on you. So you'd better get your act together and be very good at what you're going to present. The techniques of power lunching will give you power — how you use that power is up to you. The following chapters will tell you all you need to know — how to plot your strategy, how to manipulate the restaurant environment, how to stress your advantages, how to avoid common pitfalls. The practical: Whom to invite. How to select the restaurant. What to order. How much to drink. Which chair to choose. How to tip. How to get great service. When to talk business. When *not* to talk business. How to pay. How to *impress*. The full gamut of power lunching.

This approach isn't just for the "corporate man." The power lunching concept also applies to the "one-man operation," the entrepreneur. If it's one thing a one-man show needs, it's "front." You may be doing a great job running an up-and-coming business, but you wouldn't want to invite a client or prospect to your modest office. Or you may be starting a business, using rented desk space at an out-of-the-way location. Invite your client to a good power lunch restaurant and you've suddenly climbed into the same chair, the same power position as the highest-placed executive of a multinational conglomerate. You can master the power lunch game as much as anyone.

It's all here, waiting for you. Go for it!

Chapter Two

Who to Invite and How

The 3-Way, the 4-Way and Inviting the Boss

2

"Hey, Charlie," says the voice on the telephone. "Let's go get a sandwich and a beer."

In effect, that greeting answers the chapter title. Charlie is the person invited, and the method used to extend the invitation is a phone call.

It seems so simple. Actually, it's just simple-minded. In too many cases, the business lunch that has the potential of becoming a dynamic power lunch is given only this scant amount of attention.

Charlie is a guy you have done some business with. You haven't seen him for a while, and you figure a friendly get-together at lunch wouldn't hurt. Besides, it's 11 in the morning and you don't have any other lunch plans today. And, the hot-looking number in accounting keeps turning down your well-intentioned suggestions to have a bite together.

Face it: If all your business planning were as slipshod as your lunch invitation to Charlie, you'd be back in the stockroom faster than you could order the aforementioned beer.

There is, of course, an exception to that general admonition. If Charlie actually is a "good ole boy," and the only reason for the lunch is to spend some time across the table from a business contact, no real harm is done. It probably soothes your conscience and ego more than anything else. And the meals and drinks become, at least in *your* mind, a reimbursable business expense.

But if you used that informal, off-the-cuff approach in other circumstances, you would get out of the lunch exactly what you put into its planning — nothing. So let's start again with Charlie and see how some forethought can rack up points for you and your company.

THE FULL CAST

Question: Who is Charlie?

Answer: He's an executive in a decent-sized company who can directly buy what you have to sell. He's a "buyer."

Question: Who are you?

Answer: You are someone who has something to sell that Charlie can buy. Your business with Charlie has gone on for about a year, and he represents an average-sized account to you and your company. Both of you office in a good-sized metropolitan area.

Your business relationship is a good enough reason to invite Charlie to lunch. But let's invest some more thought into arranging the lunch so you will reap bigger dividends. Consider, for instance, Charlie's assistant. He does a lot of the detail work for Charlie, and knows a fair amount about your dealings with Charlie's company. Charlie is probably striving for the job of "head buyer," and his assistant could very well end up filling the void by taking Charlie's job. Should Jim, Charlie's assistant, be included in the luncheon invitation? That's the kind of question an experienced power luncher will weigh early in tailoring his tactics to the specific situation at hand.

Question: Who is Charlie's boss? In other words, who does Charlie report to directly?

Answer: Charlie answers to Mack, the head buyer, who's his immediate superior.

Now we have the full cast for a power lunch. Instead of simply dealing with one man, we now have an important chunk of the corporate hierarchy that is involved in the business you transact with Charlie's company. There's Charlie, there's his assistant, who may be responsible for developing some backup support that helps Charlie buy from you, and there's Charlie's boss, who may not even be aware of you and the services or products you sell. Except for the lunch, there probably would not be another reason for the four of you to have a meeting. And even if there were, it would be awkward to arrange and certainly wouldn't offer the potential presented by a power lunch.

Question: Will Charlie, your one solid contact in his company, have any reason to object to having his assistant and his boss at lunch with you?

Answer: Let's examine each of the additions. Jim seems to be no problem, since he's under Charlie's control and therefore poses no threat. Jim probably would enjoy the lunch, which might be a perk that he usually doesn't get. It also would provide Jim with an opportunity to become involved on a face-to-face basis as you interact with his boss. Charlie makes some brownie points with Jim by bringing him deeper into the real action. Okay for Jim.

Charlie's boss, Mack, poses a different situation. Is Charlie going to think you want to "go over his head?" That's a major concern many buyers have, and one you must recognize and deal with in planning your approach. You can alleviate Charlie's possible concern by assuring him that you would like Mack to join the luncheon meeting:

1. To accept your personal thanks for past business.
2. Because too seldom does "the boss" get to meet "the people" — those who supply his company with goods and services.

Unless Charlie feels shaky about his job security, we should be able to go ahead with including Mack.

But now that we've decided who to invite, how do you actually go about extending the invitation? "Hey, Charlie, let's go get a sandwich and a beer" isn't going to work any more.

The grammar stinks, but it can't be said more emphatically.

Right now, all your leverage is with Charlie. So let's expand your influence by adding a fine restaurant that's several notches above the sandwich-and-beer joint you might otherwise patronize with him. There may be nothing wrong with its limited menu, but the local sandwich hangout isn't going to work as an asset to help propel you into a more solid business relationship with Charlie's company. In Chapter Five, "Choosing the Restaurant," we'll detail what sort of place would be appropriate for your power lunch. First, though, let's get everyone invited.

Call Charlie on the phone and tell him you have an idea you're sure he'll like. Tell him it's been too long since you and he had a chance to meet, except by phone or briefly at his office. And although you certainly enjoy your current business relationship, it would be fine if the two of you could relax a little and discuss business in general.

Then suggest a luncheon meeting on a specific day of the following week at a restaurant that meets all *your* criteria as described in Chapter Five. Assuming Charlie agrees, he'll either propose an alternate date or accept your offer. Suggest you meet him at the restaurant, where he should simply ask for your table.

This is the time to propose expanding your luncheon cast. "Charlie," you say, "I've got another idea. I've never met your boss, Mack. I'm sure *he'll like* this restaurant, and I'd like to thank him *personally* for the business *you* have placed with me, even though you're one of the toughest buyers I've ever dealt with."

You have just set the court for your play. The restaurant is one his boss likes, and you're going to tell his boss what a good, but tough buyer he is. Everybody wins.

"Oh, Charlie," you might say at that point, "How about inviting along your assistant, Jim? I'm sure he would like to see how the big guns — like you and Mack — operate."

You haven't exactly trapped Charlie, but he's been wedged into a position in which it's easier for him to accept than reject.

"And Charlie," you say to top it off, "We'll all be back at our offices before two o'clock."

Now we know who to invite, the reasons for choosing them and essentially how to handle the invitation. Let's touch, though, on a few refinements. "Charlie, thanks for going along with the idea that the four of us get together for lunch on the fourteenth at Jeremy's," you might say. "Will you handle inviting Mack and Jim, or would you like me to call either of them directly?"

It's always a good idea to give Charlie an opportunity to put the responsibility on you for an idea he may not be totally comfortable with. It also gives Charlie a chance to back out by not inviting his boss if Charlie concludes upon reflection that it's best he attend solo.

"Great, Charlie, I'll call you Thursday morning for solid confirmation,," you say to clinch things. "I'll make the reservations in my name, and look forward to seeing all of you at noon. Remember, you're my guests."

Although you may assume Charlie knows you're paying for the meal, it's a good idea to say so specifically.

Stop now and realize what you've accomplished. Before the lunch, you had only one real contact in Charlie's company. After the lunch, you'll have three good contacts — and on three different corporate levels!

So far, we've dealt with Charlie, a buyer; his boss, Mack, the head buyer; Jim, Charlie's assistant; and yourself, a person already doing business with Charlie's company. But there's more than a bit of truth in the cliche, "The more things change, the more they remain the same." If you are:

A corporate labor attorney dealing with the personnel manager of a new client:

A director of manufacturing working with a sub-contractor;

A chief executive officer of a major financial institution working with the new director of an import-export firm;

A media representative working with an advertising agency that won't use your medium . . .

All the strategies described for setting up a power lunch apply to you, too!

Each of us, in effect, has something to sell: ourselves, our ideas, our services, our products. Power lunching is a practical, cost-effective tool to bolster our success by giving us an excellent forum to work in. As will be demonstrated here, power lunching can help you expand your contacts within an organization that you deal with. It's simply damn good business practice to do so. This gives you an opportunity to receive feedback from lower corporate levels; a chance to grow with lower and middle level managers as they grow; and the subtle but potent ability to hold the club of "being able to go to the boss" when it appears expedient.

But beware of a potential gaffe. Unless you want to lose at every client level except the very top, don't ever offer the boss a better deal than you gave those on the lower levels. You may close that one sale, but end up closing yourself out from *every* other level. Remember, middle management grows into upper management — and has a long memory.

Also, don't believe that because your prospect is such a highly placed executive in his company that you couldn't possibly invite him to a business lunch. That's ridiculous! It's like the old story of the most beautiful girl in town who sat home alone every Saturday night. She was so beautiful that all the boys thought she must be booked every night, so no one invited her out and she sat alone, alone, alone. If you feel free to talk to this executive on the phone, feel equally free to invite him to lunch. It may have been a while since *anyone* invited him, either from fear of his high position or because of the "beautiful girl syndrome." And you might find he's tired of lunching with the same clique of his peers who bring him nothing new. Every chief executive officer, president, director, vice-president, manager and buyer pulls on his pants (or she pulls on her panty hose) one leg at a time, just like everyone else. Invite them to a power lunch. You'll both gain from it.

Co-author E. Melvin Pinsel demonstrated first-hand how going to the top can bring a company a good-sized piece of new business — and develop a long-standing client. Here's his story:

A couple of years ago, an outside firm of representatives had problems selling an ad agency on the merits of using one of the radio stations we own in an upcoming advertising campaign. The agency and its client were located in Dallas, and the rep covering that territory couldn't convince the media buyer to use our station for that campaign. When I learned of the problem, I didn't phone the media buyer in Dallas from my Chicago headquarters. Instead, I called and spoke to the president of the ad agency, a man I had not met.

I didn't give him a sales pitch on the phone. Rather, I

suggested we have lunch together the next day at the then-just-opened Mansion Restaurant in Dallas. He couldn't believe I would fly to Dallas for the sole purpose of sitting with him to discuss this single deal. But when I told him I planned to fly in from Chicago in the morning and fly out that same afternoon, he got the idea I was serious and that he was important to me.

I made reservations at the restaurant by phone and, not knowing the set-up, asked the maitre d' to seat us where we could talk easily and with privacy. Thanks to my plane being an hour late, my guest arrived before I did, and was placed at a table that permitted only side-by-side seating.

I approached, introduced myself and sat down next to him. He was drinking what looked like Scotch on the rocks. I ordered the same, and while cursing the maitre d' and airline under my breath, said: "Bill, thanks for waiting. Looks like this will be a great restaurant. Every table is taken! But *this* table doesn't exactly lend itself to talking business. Let's you and I sit here, get acquainted and enjoy a good meal and a few drinks. We won't talk business. When we've finished lunch, I'll buy you an after-dinner drink in the lounge, and I'll take *all* your advertising budget for my station.

When he didn't put down his drink and walk out, I knew I had him! We did get well-acquainted, have a fine lunch and a few drinks, and didn't discuss business. After lunch, we adjourned to a quiet table in the almost-deserted lounge, where we had coffee and brandy while talking a lot of business.

No, I didn't get *all* the money, but I got a very good amount of new business. Bill and I are solid business friends today, and his media buyer listens to my rep with more respect.

Don't be afraid to go to the top!

This anecdote also illustrates another lesson of successful power lunching: Don't let an unexpected situation throw you. Mel ended up with a less-than-perfect environment for his luncheon, with the seating arrangement providing a major problem. But instead of panicking, he improvised by suggesting that the business discussion be confined to the lounge, thus maneuvering into a place where he had better control. It would have been a mistake to try wedging the business talk into the flawed surroundings of the dining room.

NEW BUSINESS

New business, of course, is vital for expanding volume and profits, as well as covering for accounts that one day will leave you or diminish in size. In seeking new business, sometimes you run up against the old excuse, "I just don't have time to see you — call me in a couple of months." Don't believe it!

If you've qualified the new business prospect to the point where you know he offers good potential, go after him this way:

"Mr. Johnson, I do understand how busy you are. But we all have to take a lunch break. Let's get together Tuesday or Thursday for a *quick* lunch meeting where we can at least get to know each other somewhat and touch on a few of the ideas I've mentioned on the phone. I do know of a good restaurant right near your office where we can talk. Which day is better for you — Tuesday or Thursday?"

It's a ploy that works more often than not!

ONE ON ONE

Obviously, everything discussed here about three-guest power lunches applies when, in your judgment, the power lunch is best handled as a two-man affair. There are many times when a one-on-one meeting is the very best way to go. Confidences can be shared with no concern that another person is aware of what transpired.

So there we have it — *who* to invite to a power lunch and *how* to do so. Remember: Invite your immediate contact. Attempt to expand the lunch to include lower and upper echelons. Cover your middle-level contact from concern about going over his head. Keep in mind that whatever business or profession is involved, the basic drives and needs are similar, as are the solutions. Go to the top when you can, and remain open to one-on-one confidences.

Bon apetite — and happy business hunting!

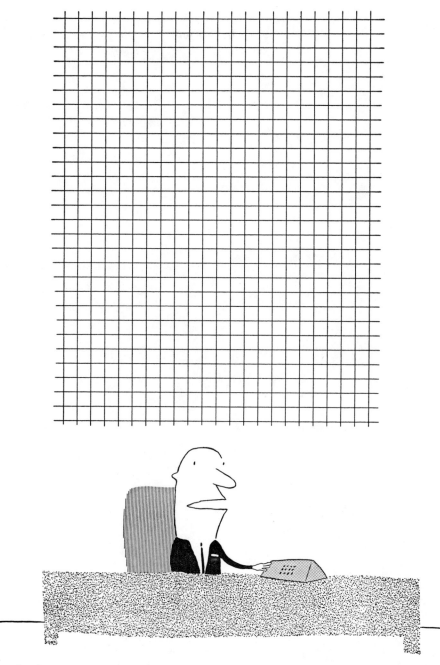

"Mary, would you set up a power lunch with the sales group from the Merbel Corporation? We'll need Meyerson for the numbers, Fletcher for his upsmanship, and Smitty to sit there and be trendy."

Planning the Strategy

Foreplay and Making Your Move

3

"I know some people," says a New York hotel executive, "who keep a book on their clients and propspective clients, running to 1,000 names: their wives' and children's names as well as their hobbies, their favorite foods, their restaurant preferences — a running record. Each time they would take someone to lunch, they would look through their book to check them out."

Few people are this meticulous, but his remark illustrates the lengths power lunchers will go to be prepared, to do their homework, *to plan their strategy!*

You wouldn't attend an important meeting without knowing (1) what you want to achieve; (2) what your client generally is willing to offer: (3) what his personality quirks are and where his soft spots are so they can be used to win him over and increase your gain; and (4) a step-by-step plan of how you will conduct the meeting.

Since a power lunch is, in short, a meeting-with-a-meal, you need at least this much preparation — and usually more because you have more props to work with and more decisions to make (such as the restaurant staff, seating, food and drink). If you prepare in advance, you can use all these tools to your advantage.

RESEARCH YOUR CLIENT.

To pass any test, you have to do your homework. When important client Hank, someone you've only met in passing, accepts your lunch invitation, don't wait until 11:45 that morning to start wondering: Does Hank like fish? Is he a vegetarian? Does he drink — one glass of wine or three martinis? Does he smoke? Is he a football fan — or does he prefer foreign films? The more answers you know to questions like these, the better-equipped you will be and the less you will leave to chance. That is, you will have more control.

"The difference between successful people and losers — they do their homework," says a top power luncher. "To have the 'edge,' it is essential to know your guest's habits."

So what do you do — hire a private detective? No, but it helps if you do a little sleuthing on your own. Even before you have telephoned Hank to invite him, you must start your research. Otherwise, how else will you even know which restaurant to select? Ask questions of anyone who knows Hank well, such as his co-workers, colleagues, even his secretary. Don't ask vague questions such as, "What is Hank like?" Instead, say, "I'm entertaining Hank, and I would like to make it as pleasant for him as possible. Can you give me some specifics about his likes and dislikes?" Usually, people will be very helpful because they're flattered that you think they're knowledgeable, observant and a good judge of human nature. And by telling them you're taking Hank to lunch, they'll know what sort of information to offer and won't be suspicious of your motives.

BREAKING BREAD TOGETHER

"There are certain people who are known as pushovers for certain kinds of lunches," says Tom Roeser, Vice-president for Government Relations at Quaker Oats. "A very prominent C.E.O. I know does just the opposite than expected. The normal thing is to go and have several martinis and an adequate lunch. This guy likes a glass of V-8 juice, maybe some cold cuts and generally a very, very spartan meal. People know him so well that those who entertain him are sometimes prepared to order this kind of lunch as well.

"So when the waiter comes over, the host will say, 'Oh, I'm an athletic guy and don't really like a heavy meal, so maybe I'll just have a glass of V-8 juice,' and this guy says, 'How wonderful that you and I agree!' When you have that kind of agreement, it sets the mood of agreement for other things."

Since imitation is the highest form of flattery, it's a very high power play to order the same thing as your guest — in food or drink. If you both drink Glenfiddich (even if you can't stand it) or broiled swordfish, it immediately puts a stamp of approval on your guest's selection, and you two already have something in common.

It's a major faux pas — a crime inexperienced lunchers often commit — to order something that's implicitly critical of your guest's selection. Let's say your guest has ordered soup, oysters and steak tartare, and you say, "I'll just have a shrimp salad." Even before you have made a comment about your diet, your guest is already humiliated because, psychologically, you are not joining him in his meal.

And unless you weigh 300 pounds, saying anything about a diet at a power lunch is an unforgivable insult. It's similar to inviting someone out for a drink and then letting the guest drink alone. What's the point? Your guest has come prepared for a lunch that is, if not a celebration, at least a "breaking of the bread together." If one of you is breaking bread and the other a celery stick, you're either an amateur and didn't do your homework or don't belong in the power lunch class.

A woman public relations executive we know was fired because she could not master this simple technique of breaking bread together. Always being on a diet — although she was usually thinner than her guests — she ordered just a salad, and succeeded not at power lunching but only in subconsciously insulting her clients.

MUTUAL INTERESTS.

Your research doesn't end when you have learned your guest's food and drink preferences. It's also a big plus to know his general interests and, if possible, his latest achievements. If your guest just received a promotion or award, mention it! If he's a magazine publisher, be sure to read the current issue. If your guest is involved in a political controversy, bone up on the facts. In all cases, your guest will be complimented and impressed with your awareness. And you will have a topic of conversation that your guest will find most flattering — himself.

"The research starts with the kind of lunch a guy eats,

and then goes to his occupation and pre-occupation, be it sports or politics," Tom Roeser advises. "If a guy sits down over power lunch and says, 'I may be wrong, C.J., and I may be violating everything you believe in, but I think President Reagan was 100 percent right in naming Henry Kissinger to this panel.' With that, C.J. will say, 'Why, I congratulate you because I feel the same way!'"

Of course, you have done enough research to know you are not taking a chance with your remark. Even so, Roeser adds, "I find that sometimes it is better to take a chance and have a guy disagree with me because it shows you're a real person."

In all cases, in order to disagree with your guest, agree with him or know what subjects to avoid, you must know where he stands. And the only way to discover that is by research.

"The whole issue is to know your customer, and know what you're trying to achieve by the luncheon," says a Houston executive, who also cautions to keep it within the bounds of your personality. "Being something you're not comes across clearly to most people, and that's when you don't sell. I've seen people that over the years have been described as 'a great salesman.' The truth was that they weren't great salesmen — they were bombastic, aggressive, strong and they *sounded* like they knew what they were talking about, but it really wasn't a personality that was desirable to most people. Sometimes, it's much better to be laid-back and soft sell."

If you're the type of person who can pull off a successful flattery routine, you will be that much ahead at a power lunch. However, don't become a blathering fool whose compliments are an obvious and obnoxious ploy.

A famous and rather pompous gourmet wine and food critic had his credibility punctured over lunch when one of his guests asked him what he thought of the Rosehall Cabernet Sauvignon 1978 — a totally fictitious wine made up at the moment. The critic, in an embarrassing attempt to keep his reputation of superior knowledge at all costs, proceeded to describe the wine at great length. With that, the critic's credibility — and his power — evaporated.

Remember: Sometimes the smartest remark you can utter is a simple: "I don't know."

"I believe in the value of being self-effacing," says a Washington, D.C., power luncher. "The reason is that your guest usually will be on their best behavior, putting on an appearance of power. I like to play it just the opposite — there are many things that I don't know, many things to learn, etc.

"I worked for a congressman once who used this ploy to his great benefit for years, was given credit for being very cagey and playing dumb. People got very suspicious to the point where, when he sat down and said, 'Well, I just don't know anything about that,' the other people usually thought, 'Oh, my God, he knows everything about it!'"

Whatever tack you take, it's sure to fail unless you've done a thorough job of investigating your guest so that your power lunch strategy has some meat on its bones. But can this research go too far? As Tom Roeser found out, sometimes it can.

"When I tried out for this job," he says, "I had breakfast with the C.E.O. of the company. I really wanted this job. I had researched the Quaker Oats Company totally, and I wanted to impress this guy very much — the chairman of the company, Bob Stuart.

"I was fairly young, and during breakfast, I was trying to show Mr. Stuart how smart I was, how much I knew about the company's sales, etc. The waiter was standing nearby and Mr. Stuart said, 'What would you like for breakfast?' And I said, 'I'll have bacon and eggs.' The waiter looked at Mr. Staurt and he said, 'I'll have oatmeal!'

"And I thought, 'Oh my God, how did I hope to get a job at the Quaker Oats Company talking about all these things and forgetting the most important thing — oatmeal.'"

Stuart, though, had a refreshing attitude. "I appreciate your candor and forthrightness," he said. "The fact that a man orders bacon and eggs with me when he's trying to get a job in an oatmeal company shows he must be very self-assured."

It was, in short, a case of researching something so well that you actually forget the most important fact of all — who you're dining with.

STAFF-UP

So far, so good. You've researched your client and know what to expect. But what if he's not coming alone?

If you're in a straightforward sales situation, a one-to-one relationship at lunch is preferrable. It keeps you on purpose and there is no fear of the effort being diluted by other people. However, sometimes others are integral to the lunch's purpose, such as if you're trying to introduce someone or bring in another viewpoint.

As discussed in the last chapter, your client may be bringing along his sales manager, ad director or media buyer. In this case, try to even things out. "You've got to balance numbers," says a New York television executive. "You shouldn't be at a disadvantage." On the other hand, if your guest is coming alone, don't bring anyone else or he might get the feeling you are ganging up on him. This holds true unless, of course, it's an introduction lunch and your guest was specifically asked to attend. Even though some people with very strong personalities may be able to take on two guests, generally it's best to be equal in number.

If more than one person is coming, though, additional preparation is needed. For instance, Jerry and Bill are partners in an ad firm. Jerry is pitching client George, who has asked that Jerry bring Bill to lunch so that he can meet both heads of the shop. At lunch, Bill and Jerry are trying hard to impress George, and both are vying for his attention. Frequently, the partners, in a subconscious effort to compete with each other, will work at cross-purposes, making errors and confusing George. They may even be signaling each other by kicks under the table and cutting off each other's conversation direction. It's like the two lawyers who were representing a single client in a Los Angeles trial a few years ago. One offered some documents into evidence, at which time his flustered partner shot to his feet and exclaimed, "I object, your honor!"

To avoid this sort of confusion at a power lunch, Jerry and Bill will have to work out their approach in advance. They must assign roles, divide responsibilities and, most important, discuss and agree on the main purpose of the lunch and by what means that goal will be achieved. *Bill and Jerry cannot have equal roles.* One will have to be the main host and lead the lunch in conversation and timing, while the other must take his cues from him. They must discuss in advance who will say what and what points they plan to avoid entirely.

PRACTICE, PRACTICE, PRACTICE

No matter how many people will attend a power lunch, it's effective preparation to mentally rehearse every segment of the upcoming encounter. Experienced power lunchers know exactly how they will arrive at the restaurant — by car or cab. Will they need singles for cab fare, doormen or car hikers? Will they need change to make telephone calls, or five and ten dollar bills for tips? How will they pay the bill? Do they have an extra credit card in case of a mixup with the first card? Don't be put into the awkward situation of reaching into your pocket and trying to tip the maitre d', only to find you have a single, two twenties, two fifties and an American Express card!

Also, mentally go through the ordering of drinks and lunch, trying to anticipate the timing of the meal, how much time you will spend on "small talk" and when you will bring up business. Imagine yourself paying — or signing — the check at the table or at the maitre d's desk, and leaving the restaurant. Will you be going the same direction as your guest and, if so, will you join him in a cab or walk with him? Or will you purposefully plan to go in a different direction? Being well-prepared has wonderful side-effects: You become relaxed, remain unruffled by unexpected irritations and are able to concentrate on the purpose of your lunch.

Sometimes, a power lunch strategy can include some tricks you wouldn't be able to pull off in an office meeting. Bob Crain, a San Francisco filmmaker, used some imaginative tactics when Sydney Hermann — pseudonym for an elderly, quarrelsome, petty and generally hard-to-get-along-with distributor — arrived to work out publicity for the opening of Crain's film in San Francisco. Crain was certain the local public relations firm could handle the job best, but Hermann was skeptical and insisted he meet the principals at lunch. Crain arranged the lunch and invited the three P.R. agents —

two women and a man — and Hermann. Crain's scheme was to tone down Hermann's rambunctiousness and persuade him to accept the firm.

In a stroke of genius, instead of taking a cab to the restaurant, Crain told Hermann they were going to a place within walking distance. What Hermann didn't know was that this meant the restaurant was eight blocks away — up and down San Francisco's hills. When they arrived at the restaurant, Hermann was huffing and puffing, with most of his fighting spirit dissipated. Crain seated the worn-out Hermann between the two very attractive P.R. women and, after lunch, they got the account.

Remember, a power lunch is, in short, a meeting-with-a-meal. And just as any smart businessman will plan his strategy for an important office meeting, so will he check *all* the details before his power lunch. Planning, strategy, power . . . success!

Chapter Four

The Woman Invites

How to Have Him
Eating Out of Your Hand

4

For women, power lunching with a man presents an entire menu of unique problems. The trick to turning lunch into a profitable business experience is knowing where these pitfalls are hidden — and how to transform them into opportunities.

Some matters that are straightforward for men can raise subtle but difficult obstacles for female executives. When Joe Smith calls up Charlie Jones of Worldwide Widgets and invites him to lunch, Charlie faces only one general concern: "Will Joe try selling me something? If I buy, will this be in my company's best interest? Or is Joe trying to put over a fast one?"

Yet if *Mary* Smith invites Charlie Jones to lunch, Charlie asks himself two additional questions that arise from his own tradition-encrusted male attitudes: "Is she making a pass at me?" And: "Should I make a pass at her?"

The bottom line is that Mary needs to be twice as skillful at lunch as Joe.

Sound difficult? It doesn't have to be. You, as a woman, can overcome this handicap — but *only* if you maintain power before, during and at the end of your lunch encounter. To do that, you — not Charlie Jones — must call *all* the shots.

Since freedom is the opportunity to choose, it's clearly to your advantage to eliminate as many of your male guest's choices as you can. This limits his freedom and puts him in your power. So *you* must decide when and where to lunch, where you will sit, what you will eat, how long you will dine and how much to tip. In sum, *all* the important decisions are yours. Otherwise, the power will flow to your male guest — a shift that would sap your effectiveness.

MY PLACE OR YOURS?

Planning the successful power lunch must begin *before* you pick up the telephone to invite your guest. Figure out details about the lunch in advance because once you're on the phone, you must confidently state the date, time and place for the meeting. Again, you're eliminating his choices. Once you have an agreement to meet at, say, noon Thursday, only your rudest guest would decline your choice of place. So your call should go something like this: "Why don't we have lunch next Thursday, if you're free?" If the answer is affirmative, clinch the engagement by saying: "12 o'clock at Randall's. I'll meet you there."

You've already scored three power points by eliminating his choices — which may not have been 12 o'clock or Thursday or Randall's. So you're ahead even before the appetizers are ordered.

But be sure to map your strategy carefully. For a businesswoman, there is nothing better than a highly respected restaurant where you are known by the staff and are treated as an important business person. You should be recognized by the maitre d', called by name and given a preferential table. Successful women have three or four of these favorite spots in reserve, preferably serving different cuisine — French, seafood, steaks, for example — to avoid monotony.

Just because you may be comfortable with several places, however, don't make the mistake of asking your guest, "Would you prefer Carson's or the Consort Room?" To keep your power, *you* must decide *each time*.

Successful power lunches also match their guest to the restaurant they select. If you don't know your guest well, try choosing the lunch site based on his profession, proximity of the restaurant to *his* office and his likes and dislikes. For instance, if he's an advertising executive, choose the "in" spot for those in his occupation. You can also do some research into your guest's preferences by calling someone who knows him or even asking his secretary. You might say, "I'm entertaining Mr. Vanderbilt at lunch, and I'd like to make the occasion as pleasing as possible for him. Can you tell me a little about what he enjoys?" Such inquiries can yield valuable tidbits of intelligence, including the type of restaurant he prefers and whether he smokes or drinks. Knowledge is power, and the more information you collect about your power lunch guest, the greater your command.

Beware, though, of one gaping pitfall in selecting your power lunch restaurant. Women should *always* avoid the enchanting little French cafe where their boyfriend or husband took them to dinner. The reasons: Not only will the romantic atmosphere flare Charlie's suspicions about the "real" purpose for your lunch, but you will be treated by the restaurant staff as the wife of Mr. Y, rather than being known as *the* person in power. In other words, you will be treated politely, but won't be given the deference and respect of the person who pays the bill and tips the staff.

In fact, many savvy businesswomen purposefully avoid taking their husbands or boyfriends to their favorite business lunch haunts. "Otherwise, it only confuses the staff members, who are used to seeing me with a client when I pay the tab," says a highly placed woman advertising executive. "When my husband tries to pay, they find this unusual, and if affects my predictability and power position in the restaurant."

Then there's the unusual occasion when being known in a restaurant can actually go too far. Such was the case when business executive Sally Berger, wife of Miles Berger, an owner of Chicago's Mayfair Regent Hotel, was lunching at Ciel Bleu, which sits atop the building.

On the restaurant's menu, among other things, was a Norman Omelet, a Sally Salad — and Miles Burger. While Sally was entertaining a male client one day, they overheard five elderly woman chatting at a nearby table. First woman: "What's a Miles Burger?" Second woman: "Oh, he's one of the owners of the hotel." Third woman: "Very friendly with ex-Mayor Byrne, isn't he?" Fourth woman: "Who would eat a Miles Burger?" Fifth woman: "Probably only his wife!" Sally smiled through the entire conversation — until the last line. "Well, that's pretty impressive, Sally," her guest concluded.

"What do you do for an encore?"

Other places high on the list to avoid: Restaurants with a large share of banquette (side by side bench) seating, dimly lit male bastions and clubs — unless it's your own. Obviously, it's a disaster to lunch at someone else's club, no matter how prestigious, because you've lost *all* your power. You probably wouldn't even know where the ladies' room is. As for darkened restaurants, there's the danger they will ignite Charlie's lust, and your chances of getting a decent table at a restaurant that has a lot of banquette seating are slim. Naturally, you don't want to be seated side-by-side with your male guest because you're in danger of trading the all-important business "eye contact" for the instant power-destroying "thigh contact."

FEATHERING THE NEST.

Like any successful business meeting, a business lunch takes planning. Now that Charlie has agreed to meet you at Randall's, you must continue cutting off his choices at the pass (we'll talk later about how to cut off his passes). First, call Pierre, the maitre d' at Randall's, to make your reservation. If you are established at the restaurant as you should be, you won't have trouble getting your favorite table.

Take advantage of this time to arrange for Pierre to let you sign the check away from your guest's view. Pierre will accomplish this by approaching your table after coffee service and saying, "Miss Smith, there's a telephone call for you." Translation: Your check is ready to sign. Of course, when you enter the restaurant, you slip Pierre your American Express card and a tip. The cash is intended to keep Pierre's memory sharp enough to remember your "telephone call." When you return to Charlie after signing the check, you're radiant with victory because the choice of paying the check is no longer his.

This foolproof method of handling the check situation is used not only by women, but by a great number of male power lunchers as well. Even so, some professional women we interviewed say they encounter no trouble when paying the check at the table, thanks primarily to changing attitudes toward business women.

"I'd say 99 percent of my clients are men, and this is never a problem," says Cher Patric, vice president at Aaron Cushman Public Relations. "If I have a client who might be older and more traditional, I would just tell him in advance that I would like him to be my guest for lunch — just set it up so that there are no surprises and no awkwardness. I think that the problem might exist for a younger account person with a paternal client who thinks that he doesn't have money, but not for a woman who's been in business for a number of years and is used to wheeling and dealing."

So if you're experienced at lunching and are confident about being able to handle the check smoothly at the table, go ahead. But if you have an older or "macho" guest or you're very young, the safest way is still to make arrangements to sign the check away from the table. Remember, it's best to leave nothing to chance at a power lunch.

WHERE TO MEET.

Charlie has agreed to meet you for lunch at Randall's. Okay, but exactly where do you meet? In the bar? In the foyer? Or at the table?

Remember, our goal is to eliminate Charlie's opportunities to choose. Meeting in the bar might seem innocent enough, but it's a disaster when Charlie arrives and you need to move to a table. That's because there's the bar tab to deal with. When ill at ease, men will fall back on their traditional behavior with women, and this means Charlie will have the opportunity to reach for your check — and your power. Don't let him. (If this should happen, however, take the tab and ask the bartender to transfer it to your dining check. Don't make a big deal out of it.)

Waiting in the foyer is even worse because it gives Charlie the chance to exercise another male tendency — taking you by the arm, approaching the maitre d' and perhaps even asking for a table of *his* choice. Of course, you must understand Charlie's plight. If he doesn't take your arm or select the table, his upbringing tells him he has lost his masculinity. He may simply be doing what he thinks is expected of him — if you leave the choice to him.

What's the best way to eliminate Charlie's choices so you can maintain power? Meet him at the table of *your* choice. Arrive early, check your coat and be seated. When Charlie arrives, he will be shown to your table.

He and the power are *yours*.

SHEEP'S CLOTHING.

You've got him where you want him. He's your one-man audience, and you have his complete attention. What kind of an impression are you making on him — not just with your conversation, but through the way you've dressed? For years, businessmen have been chided for wearing drab, unimaginative clothing. Yet there's a good reason for this: It leaves nothing for an opponent to criticize. Even after mastering the rules of power, some women bungle it all by arriving at lunch wearing red stockings, the latest "trendy" outfit, jangling jewelry and talon nails. To pull off the power lunch, you can't distract your prey. Subtlety and "sheep's clothing" are the key.

Maintaining power during lunch requires a woman to dress conservatively, projecting an image of being ready for business. And your purse is especially crucial. One sure way to receive power demerits is to mishandle your handbag. Asked to produce a business card, pen or appointment calendar, many otherwise successful women dive into their large pouch, stir its contents for a while and lose all credibility and power when they can't come up with what they were after. So before leaving for lunch, check to see where your cards, pen, calendar and American Express card are located, and make sure you can retrieve them in a hurry when they're needed.

A final no-no for a woman of power is make-up repair at the table. Compacts and lipstick remind Charlie of his primping wife or girlfriend, and suddenly you'll find yourself pictured in his mind as a member of a subservient group.

TIME FOR TIMING

With timing so crucial to a power lunch, make certain you orchestrate everything in advance with the maitre d' and the captain. For instance, you might say something like this to the maitre d' before Charlie arrives: "When we sit down, please take the drink order. Then ask the captain to leave Mr. Jones and me alone for 20 minutes. Bring the menus only when I signal for them." This ensures the captain will be looking for *your* signal — not Charlie's — and that you and Charlie will have 20 minutes to get acquainted without interruption by menus or a recitation of "specials." And most important, the maitre d' and captain will know you're taking active charge of the meal.

This makes ordering easier after you and Charlie are seated. When the maitre d' or captain asks if you'd like a drink, immediately turn to Charlie and say, "What would you like?" Charlie might reply, "Manhattan on the rocks, please." While you may not quite be able to get in the phrase, "The gentleman would like . . . ," at least you have forced Charlie to order first and preempted him from saying, "The lady would like . . . ," a sexist cliche whose "lunch with a girlfriend" connotation has no place at a power lunch. When ordering food, follow the same format. As soon as the captain arrives, turn to Charlie and say, "What have you decided on?"

Having done your homework on Charlie, you should know if, what and how much he drinks, and whether he is a light or robust luncher. The polite power lunch ploy is to take your cue from your guest. For instance, if Charlie is a nondrinker, you must abstain or have only one drink. If Charlie is an appetizer-entree-dessert man, you must match his order course for course, even if you'd actually prefer only a small salad. (After all, you can just take small bites of everything!)

Remember: A power lunch focuses on business and power, not on your personal preferences or waistline. In the power lunch arena, your motivation isn't hunger, it's building Charlie's self-esteem in order to put over your business deal.

HEAR NO EVIL.

Words carry weight at a power lunch. Conversation, in short, is the ultimate test of who's in charge. You may have selected the time, date and place with skill and aplomb, but what do you talk about now that you've got Charlie where you want him — sitting across from you, drink in hand?

Keep in mind that a power lunch is not a date with a girlfriend, which means 90 percent of your usual conversation is taboo. Keep the small talk interesting, but impersonal. Discuss his industry, company or business goals. Also on the "safe" list: current world and local affairs, politics, entertainment, sports, travel and pets. Avoid talking about sex, women's liberation, children, divorces, dates, lovers, spouses, psychiatrists, personal problems, fashion and make-up. If he brings up any of these subjects, cut him off at the pass by rerouting the topic back to a less personal area.

In today's climate of increased freedom for women, the male tale of woe has changed from "My wife doesn't understand me" to "My wife has left me" — and often not just "me," but the children, dog and cat as well. As Zorba says, "The whole catastrophe!"

Guard against letting any businessman confide personal problems to you. This reduces your role from a respected business person to a stand-in Ann Landers. If you allow him to fill your ear with his personal matters, you will have gained a "buddy" — but lost a power lunch.

HE WHOSE BREAD I EAT IS WHOSE SONG I SING.

Even though you've finessed the check-paying problem like a veteran power luncher, you must act carefully to prevent Charlie from chipping away at your dominance. As a woman, you've got to pay for *everything* to maintain power. Many female executives succeed in paying an expensive tab, only to botch the power lunch by letting their male guest tip the coat-check person and foot the cab fare back to the office. The result: A drain on the reservoir of power points they've accumulated during their otherwise well-executed meal.

Let's say you've paid the lunch bill, and you and Charlie are getting up to leave. Before departing the table, pull out your coat check tab and a dollar bill so you can hand both to the attendant before Charlie can offer to "take care of it." It's all right if Charlie offers to hold your coat for you because, if all has gone as planned, you're still in power and he has been won over.

There's a major difference between Charlie trying to pay

the lunch tab and offering to hold your coat, open the door for you and light your cigarette. Those are civilized courtesies that don't diminish your power. Money is the name of the game. After paying the expenses and benefiting from all the power that accrues from that, only the most immature businesswoman would muddle the situation by initiating a debate on women's rights. On the other hand, some women power lunchers light cigarettes and hold coats for their clients. It usually depends on which person has the matches or the free hands. In either case, it's a mistake to make a big deal out of it.

There's one last monetary hurdle as you and Charlie exit the restaurant. Charlie will inevitably offer to drop you off in a cab — and pay for it. Don't let him. Say you're going in a different direction. Thank him for lunch and stride off.

TO SUM UP.

Remember, a woman needs to be twice as skillful at a power lunch as a man if she is to be as successful. Social and business attitudes, slow to change, have placed many additional obstacles in her way and she must be aware of what they are and how they can be overcome. The subject of sexual awareness, one of the major obstacles, is discussed in greater detail in Chapter 12.

Choosing the Restaurant

Making the Power Choice

5

Initially, the hundreds of restaurants clammoring for your business in any major city seem hopelessly overwhelming. Do you flip through the local dining guide and simply throw a dart? Do you go to the unassuming pizza place closest to your office or to the pretentious revolving rooftop restaurant where there is a fresh maitre d' every day and the rolls seem to have been there for months? Or do you just give up and go to the trendy place that you saw mentioned in last week's paper — only to discover that it's on the cutting edge of haute cuisine and specializes in squid with strawberry sauce-puree?

Or do you resort to the ultimate cop-out and lose all power by calling your guest and asking him where he would like to go?

Remember that in selecting the location for your power lunch, you are choosing a place where you will be conducting a very important business meeting. Just as in any crucial business presentation, the more control you have over everything and the less you leave to chance, the greater likelihood of success. With this in mind, your choices narrow rapidly.

YOU MUST DECIDE!

So the first rule is that *you* — not your wife, mistress, mother, lover and especially *not* your client — must select the restaurant. How else can you be in control?

One New Yorker found out how easily power can be lost when he asked his guest whether he would prefer a luxurious East Side luncheon spot or an old-time hangout for prominent politicians. The guest opted for the fancy locale. The host was dismayed because at the political restaurant, he could have introduced his guest to powerful people. But they ended up attending a restaurant three times as expensive instead of one that was three times as powerful. Both the host and the guest lost, with the host forfeiting most of all — and ending up paying an expensive bill as well.

The lesson: never give your guest a choice. Simply say: "one o'clock at 21."

GO WHERE YOU ARE KNOWN

Rule Number Two is that it's essential to patronize restaurants where you are known. This means that everyone from the doorman to the maitre d', and even the hat-check person, will greet you by name. If there are fellow diners who are important to your industry or profession that stop by to say hello, so much the better. The instant recognition bolsters your credibility and elevates you in your guest's opinion.

Restaurant experts and frequent power lunchers agree that being known in a restaurant is the single most important element in selecting your power lunch location. Says Lee Gottlieb, Senior Vice-President and Group Supervisor for Aaron Cushman Public Relations and a successful power luncher for more than 20 years: "The maitre d' should greet you by name. 'Hello, Mr. Gottlieb, your usual table?' But this does not come easy. You have to work at it and, alas, even pay for it.

"I periodically see that the maitre d' receives some recognition for his services in the form of a $10 bill discreetly enclosed in a handshake. Doing this several times a year, in addition to Christmas, guarantees the recognition you desire.

"Also," he continues, "by going to a place habitually, chances are that you will see people there who you know, and who know you. So, as you are walking to your table, you're greeted by people. 'Hi, Lee, how are you?' Your client or prospect, of course, is aware of this, which adds to your prestige.

"When you sit down, you can also comment on some of the celebrities in your field who are also there. 'There's Irv

Kupcinet.' Or, 'There's Dan Rather.'"

Maitre d' Jean Pierre Sire agrees with Gottlieb. "You have to get yourself known by the staff before you can impress anyone."

Jean Pierre says there are two ways to become known in a restaurant: "By being a good tipper and a class person or just the opposite, by being a disagreeable bum. If you are the latter, you should never come back again."

Once you become known — positively, of course — the benefits multiply because you have gained admittance to an elite group. "We know by name about 75 percent of our customers," says Jean Pierre, who presides over power lunches at nationally known Chez Paul. "Everyone knows each other, and it's almost like a club."

Since there are so few good business restaurants in most large cities, you always have to book in advance, according to a large advertising agency president. That's why it's even more important to build the recognition factor with the owner or maitre d'. In a last-minute situation, you can still get in. It also helps to know the public relations person for that restaurant. They usually will be able to squeeze you in — but remember, you're using up a favor.

How do you establish a relationship with a maitre d'? "The best way to make a good impression with a maitre d' is to come in for lunch — not a power lunch, but a social lunch," Jean Pierre suggests. "This should be with a co-worker, not a spouse, to maintain the business aspect. Introduce yourself to the maitre d', give him your card and tell him you will be entertaining there frequently. And if I see that customer at least once a week, he soon becomes part of the house."

For a maitre d' to get to know you, it's essential to come often. But here's a tip: By visiting a restaurant eight times in one month, you will have a bigger impact toward becoming known than if you went once a month for a year.

Also, this can be an expensive investment in your future. If you really can't afford to be well-known in four or five restaurants, it's better to limit yourself to two or three where you are always recognized and where you can go frequently. Finally, since the relationship you establish with those restaurants is crucial to your future business dealings, you must *work* at keeping up your relationship. *This means going repeatedly, even if you don't have a power lunch.* And don't forget to stop in soon after returning from traveling.

KNOW THE LAY OF THE LAND

You should become thoroughly familiar with the restaurant, its menu, seating, hours of operation, reservations, procedures — and don't forget the location of the restrooms and public telephones (or the availability of table phones). "You must be familiar with the menu, prices, atmosphere, staff and where everything is located in order to eliminate the unexpected," says maitre d' Arturo Petterino.

Being familiar with the restaurant not only means you can give your guest directions if he needs to make a telephone call, but it also means you'll be more relaxed and comfortable because your confidence will be greater.

IN A CRISIS

What if you haven't established a relationship with a restaurant and you are in a panic because you have a power lunch coming up. Here's what a knowledgeable Los Angeles executive recommends: Have your secretary call and describe you in very important, glowing terms, such as, "The man I work for is a giant in the X industry and he is entertaining a very important client. He recognizes good service and will reward the staff accordingly, but he must have the window table."

She can even go so far as to say that if he doesn't get this table, her boss is dead forever. The theory is that since you obviously have no clout to begin with, you don't really have anything to lose. They may even buy the line!

UNCHARTERED WATERS

Power lunches, though, don't always take place in your territory. In fact, you may often be called upon to power lunch an important client in another city. Again, the key is preparation. Before leaving, call another power luncher familiar with the city you are visiting and ask for some suggestions. If time allows, try to personally check out the top two recommendations. Choose one, introduce yourself to the maitre d', check the seating and menu, make reservations and discuss the importance of the lunch. At this time, it might be wise to slip a $10 bill to the maitre d' to seal your budding relationship and ensure he will remember you when you arrive to power lunch with your guest.

A word here about tipping the maitre d'. It is not necessary to tip on every occasion. However, once you have tipped $10 you must keep it at $10 or nothing. If you increase your tip to $20 (for special favors on a specific occasion) you can never go back to $10. Any decrease in your tip can signify your displeasure with some aspect of the service. Thus, rather than move up to $20 and be stuck at that level, better to keep it at $10 and simply tip more frequently.

Lee Gottlieb relates a successful out-of-town ploy that could serve as an example to other power lunchers. "At one time I, as an executive from the Midwest, had to power lunch at a restaurant in Washington that did not take any reservations. I called them and said, "I understand you don't take reservations. My client is (and I named the head of a billion-dollar corporation). I'm meeting this client and someone from a major network in Washington. I don't want to be embarrassed in front of my client, so could you please make an exception to your 'no reservations' rule and take care of me?'"

As a result, he got his table and scored power points with his Washington client, who remarked, "I know they don't take reservations here. How did you do this?"

That's one illustration, by the way, of how a veteran power luncher was able to pull off a coup at a restaurant that otherwise wouldn't qualify as a dependable power lunch site. Power lunchers should avoid restaurants that don't take reservations because otherwise too much is left to chance.

A New York real estate executive has some other suggestions. "What I will do is call the restaurant and tell them who I am. For instance, I'll tell them I'm building the New Hyatt in town and I need a favor. Or since I know a lot of other landlords and developers, in the city, I can usually call the owner of the building where the restaurant is located."

So if you find yourself in such a situation, use your wits. Try to think of someone, anyone who has a connection with the maitre d' or owner. Any pull is better than going in cold!

NO MONKEY BUSINESS

A crucial criterion in selecting a power lunch restaurant is that it must cater to business lunches. This severely narrows your choices because when you consider restaurants where you are known and which cater *primarily* to a business lunch clientele, you will usually be able to name only five places — ten to fifteen at the most for New York's top power lunchers.

Why is it important to select a restaurant that has a reputation for business lunches? Well, if you needed a tax attorney, you wouldn't hire a divorce lawyer, even if you liked the divorce chap better and he was your old school buddy. Similarly, always choose facilities that will most effectively help you in conducting your power lunch, even though you may personally prefer the ribs at Sam's. Power lunch is business, and you must select the restaurant with an eye to its efficiency and not to your palate.

What should you look for? Acceptance of most major credit cards, smooth handling of reservations, greetings to you by name and excellent, unobtrusive service. As Arturo Petterino puts it: "The essence of good service is never having to ask for anything. The way you can tell the professionalism of the restaurant is that you don't have to worry about the service."

You should also check the table layout, making sure there is enough room between tables for privacy and not too much banquette — or side-by-side — seating, which is a disaster for power lunching.

On the other hand, sometimes it's easier to illustrate the things that immediately disqualify a restaurant for power lunching. For instance, cross the restaurant off your list if a waiter materializes at the table saying, "Hi, My name is Mike, and I'm your waiter." This is an instant indication of nonprofessionalism, according to Petterino, and usually means the waiters are actors or dancers. After all, it's such an

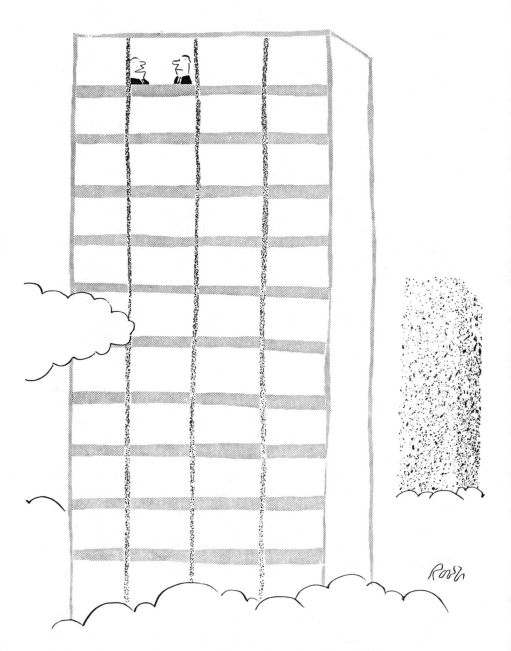

"Somehow, I can never really 'business lunch' unless I'm at least eighty floors up."

irrelevant intrusion into your professional life. Can you imagine going to the pharmacy and being told by the man at the counter, "Hi! My name is Bruce, and I'm your druggist!

Also eliminate from the power category any restaurant with hanging ferns, fashion shows or other entertainment, sidecarts with flaming dishes and recently opened establishments. It takes at least six months for a restaurant to "shake down," or get out all the quirks, after its debut. So why jeopardize your power lunch by dining there during that period?

Finally, avoid any restaurant where you have had a bad experience, such as an outstanding bill or where the maitre d' is your girlfriend's ex-husband or ex-lover. One Miami publishing executive had to reluctantly eliminate his favorite lunch spot from his power lunch list after the maitre d' lost a great deal of money in a business deal with the executive's brother. "I didn't know if he'd actually take out his anger at me," the executive said. "But I wasn't going to take any chances. I couldn't afford the gamble."

To be a successful power luncher, you should always be on the lookout for new power restaurants that might provide you with an even-better environment for furthering your business interests. To do this, take recommendations from your business friends and colleagues about new spots, but be sure to *first check them out thoroughly before inviting a business guest.* Also, don't hesitate to stop attending a restaurant that once was a great power lunch site if you notice that service has seriously deteriorated over a period of time or some other major problem has developed that could harm the business you transact there. Try first, though, to salvage the situation by discussing the problem with the maitre d' or owner to find out if corrective action will be taken. After all, you have an investment in the restaurant, too.

TO SEE AND BE SEEN

Another criterion in finding your restaurant is whether it suits your guest's profession, industry or interests. "I would not go to a fancy or pretentious restaurant the first time out. Match the restaurant to the person you're hosting," a Boston advertising executive advises. Of course, if you are power lunching with someone in the spirits, hotel or restaurant industry, more elaborate places might be in order. "The more you make your guest feel important, the more successful you will be," says Arturo Petterino, maitre d' for 38 years.

One of the primary objects of lunch is to go out in a selected atmosphere where you and your guest will be acknowledged by your peers and people who are important to your industry. This is exactly the reason why certain restaurants all get the advertising types, others the journalists and others the stockbrokers.

KNOW WHAT A RESTAURANT IS KNOWN FOR

In Chicago, it would be a disaster for a businessman to entertain a political connection at Riccardo's, which is filled with journalists. The two of you could be uncomfortable discussing impending business which you might then read about in the next day's editions. You would be better off taking him to Eli's, which is known as a restaurant where politicians are not only welcome, but where political greats from opposing camps sit side-by-side at tables and give the impression of "how well we can get along."

The main point is still to be acknowledged. At a political restaurant like Eli's, even the *enemies* acknowledge and therefore validate each other.

BE NEAR YOUR GUEST

In our effort to eliminate the unexpected in planning a power lunch, it's advisable as much as possible to select a restaurant that is closer to your guest than to you. You may have followed all the power lunch guidelines, but if your guest has to travel 20 miles on the freeway and his car has a flat tire along the way, he will not only arrive late, but blame it all on you because you suggested the arrangement. The rule is the farther your guest has to travel, the greater chance something could go wrong that is totally out of your control. Plus, it's simply good manners to make things as convenient as possible for your guest.

For example, if your office is on Wall Street in Manhattan and your client's company is located in the upper

East side, don't select a Wall Street location. If your client has offices in the suburbs, you should treat the situation like going to another city and take your client to one of the business lunch restaurants with which you have familiarized yourself in the area.

In rare cases, it's acceptable to send a limousine to pick up your guest. But you must be careful not to overpower him. A rule of thumb is that if your client is used to limousine service — and for some Californians and celebrities, it's the only way to travel — then it's perfectly all right. But you must never ride in the limo with your client. It's much more impressive to send a driver to deliver your client to the restaurant where you are already stationed. And one more point: Check out the limousine service you'll be using. A rude driver or poorly maintained vehicle can place you in a power point deficit even before your guest has walked into the restaurant.

WHEN TO GO TO A CLUB

In most major American cities, club entertaining has diminished over the years. Yet some cities are still known as "club towns."

There are pros and cons about selecting a club for a power lunch. On the plus side, clubs give you status, prestige and show you are accepted in the community. On the other hand, most clubs in the past have been — and some still are — exclusionary, discriminating against women and limiting themselves to members of certain ethnic and religious groups. Therefore, unless you know for certain that your guest will feel comfortable in your club, opt for a restaurant. And, of course, you would never agree to go to your client's club, where your power would be nil.

HOTELS AND ETHNIC RESTAURANTS

There are a few good restaurants in hotels, but generally hotel eateries should be avoided because they attract more than the usual number of conventioneers and out-of-towners. Consequently, the staff doesn't need to strive to please a steady and regular clientele, and service might be unpredictable.

Also, ethnic and foreign-flavored restaurants should be selected for power lunches only with great care, and only if you have done enough research to know your client's tastes well. Do not assume that if your client is Mexican, you should automatically take him to a Mexican restaurant. Usually, the last thing a visitor wants is his native cuisine. It's more likely he will want American food. Also, you may have looked into your client's tastes well enough to know he likes, for exampl;e, oriental food, but you could still end up displeasing him. The reason: There are differing styles of oriental cooking and you could take him to a place that fixes its dishes in a manner your guest doesn't enjoy. Ethnic restaurants should be saved for special occasions such as an evening when you are trying to show the diversity of your city to a visitor.

REMEMBER

Remember to keep in mind the following points when selecting a restaurant;
1) *You* must make the decision
2) Go where you are known
3) If you are not known . . . get known
4) Select a restaurant close to your guest
5) Establish a relationship with the maitre 'd
6) Learn the lay of the land
7) Limit your restaurant selection to those which cater to business clientele.
8) Use care in selecting either hotel or ethnic restaurants.

Chapter Six

Your Assistants:

The Restaurant Staff

Jacques, Pierre . . . and Jose

6

When you're conducting a meeting in your office, your receptionist stops drop-in visitors, your secretary screens and holds your calls and your assistants stand ready to obtain any data that might facilitate your meeting's successful outcome. Oh, yes, that's natural, you say, because you employ them and they are paid to help further your business interests.

Savvy power lunchers are keenly aware they have another team of business assistants who are just as willing, and just as professionally trained, to help them pull off their business deals. They're the service staffers in top restaurants, and they're extremely experienced in helping executives achieve their goals by making them look good in front of their clients.

How do you go about making optimal use of these assistants? According to noted restaurateur and educator Gordon Sinclair, you must take responsibility for what you want to have happen at a lunch. "If you want nothing to go wrong in a restaurant, and if your life depended on it, you would behave differently than if you were just on a social lunch with somebody."

At a power lunch, you have a definite business purpose. But if you're unfamiliar with how a restaurant operates or you're uncomfortable with using six pieces of silverware, then you will be off-purpose, concentrating on something else and leaving your business matters to chance, according to Sinclair. "A successful power lunch doesn't happen by crossing your fingers and hoping," he says. "It happens

71

because you are being fully intent on taking responsibility for what will happen."

When you're fully focused on achieving your purpose, you will get to know the restaurant, ask the maitre d' about the menu and try to get him aligned with you, Sinclair says. In essence, only when you are familiar and comfortable with the restaurant's staff and structure are you able to make best use of the team of assistants that fine eating establishments offer.

THE MAITRE D' — YOUR SECRET V.P. OF PUBLIC RELATIONS

Power lunchers and restaurant industry experts agree that a well-established relationship with the service team's leader — the maitre d' — is a top priority. "A good maitre d' knows your temperaments, likes and dislikes, and is able to work with you," says Arturo Petterino, who has probably overseen as many power lunch deals as anyone during his nearly four-decade career in Los Angeles, Palm Springs and Chicago.

According to Arturo, top power lunchers always contact him directly when making reservations. They explain the purposes of the lunch, as well as their desires for seating, timing and even menu specials. Then he is able to anticipate their needs and will assign the captain and waiter he feels are best tailored to the client's needs.

It's no wonder when an exceptional maitre d' leaves one restaurant for another, a huge clientele usually follows him. This isn't because they necessarily like his personality or sense of humor. It's because they know he is a professional and no matter where he goes, he is familiar with their mode of operation, will continue to recognize them and will always assist them in making their power lunches succeed.

Remember, a maitre d' commands a potent arsenal that he can launch into action to aid you whenever necessary. Depending on the restaurant's size, he has at least three captains, nine waiters and numerous bus boys at his disposal. He can, in special circumstances, summon them all to cater to a special client. This doesn't happen often, but it does demonstrate the artillery available to a maitre d' in the power lunch arena.

You've got to learn to show these guys who's boss.
Then you'll get great service like I do.

It's not surprising the maitre d' is generally dictator of the dining room, even to the point that the manager and owner usually abide by his decisions. After all, only he holds those tenuous and personal relationships with clients — relationships that can either break or build a restaurant's reputation.

PLACING THE RESERVATION

So establish a rapport with the maitre d' and, most important, ask to speak to him when making reservations. "The maitre d' *wants* that special contact — that is why he is there," Arturo says. "He cannot always answer the phone personally because he has other things to do. But if you have a power lunch coming up, don't give your reservation to the receptionist. It's the maitre d' you should ask for."

Nick Nicholas, flamboyant owner of Nick's Fishmarket restaurants in Houston and Chicago (which have been cited by Esquire magazine as top business luncheon spots in those cities) agrees the most successful business people call him or his maitre d' directly. When making the reservation, they also will arrange for special details, such as a certain table, a phone jack and even menu selections. Some will even say, "Mr. Smith does not want a lot of people around the table." *Indeed, the more details you provide the maitre d' when placing your reservation, the more he and his staff will be in tune with you. He can't help you if you don't let him.*

Failing to inform the maitre d' of essential details can cause an entire luncheon to go awry — as an executive we'll call Fred Hanson discovered. Fred, an executive at a large bank, made reservations for two at noon in the name of "Hanson." His guest, let's call her Sharon Smith, a vice president of finance for a large auto leasing firm, arrived on time, but didn't see Fred, who unfortunately was late. While Sharon scanned the room for her host, two executives from Fred's competing bank recognized her and invited her to join them for a drink while she was waiting. Of course, Fred was aghast when he finally arrived and saw his guest being, if not power lunched, at least "power cocktailed" by his competition! Even after Sharon left her temporary friends, this lunch was never the same. Fred's power had been short-circuited.

How did Fred manage to plunge a potential power lunch into the wimp category even before sitting down at the table? Well, first Fred didn't let the maitre d' assist him by telling him the name of his guest (and, in this case, perhaps a description may have been in order). This would have allowed the maitre d' to intercede and "guard" Sharon, either by seating her at Fred's reserved table or by stationing her in the foyer (or even the bar) with a reassuring explanation that her host would arrive any minute. In short, Fred failed to let the maitre d' work *with* him.

Second, in a power lunch, he who is late loses. That's especially true of the host, who absolutely cannot be late or he risks losing everything — even his client! Being on time, or preferably early, gives the host an opportunity to check with the maitre d' on the choice of captain, table and seating. And if he wants to change any of these things, he can do so without having his guest witness it. This is all "backstage" maneuvering that you will want to shield from your guest in a power lunch.

Okay, so let's start again.

"Good morning, Four Seasons."

"Good morning. May I speak with Pierre, please . . .

"Good morning, Pierre. This is Bob Johnson. I'm entertaining a client from Germany at lunch tomorrow. His name is Hans Schmidt. We will arrive at one. Could we please have the first table and be out by 3 p.m.? Also, I'd like to sign the check at the desk away from my guest."

This informative reservation gives the maitre d' all the necessary facts: The lunch's purpose, the table location, the time frame and how the check will be handled. The maitre d' then goes into action. He decides upon the captain (perhaps one fluent in German), relays the purpose of your lunch to his staff and advises them of the time limit.

Bob Johnson makes it a point to arrive at the Four Seasons a few minutes in advance of his guest so he can determine if everything is in order and if the table he requested is indeed the table he wants. He then will select his power seat at the table (more on that in later chapters) and tell the maitre d' where he wants Schmidt seated when he arrives.

The maitre d', for his part, will have primed the staff to cater to Johnson's needs. If Johnson is delayed for some reason, Pierre will give Schmidt a plausible explanation and save the day.

HOW TO TELL THE REDS FROM THE BROWNS . . . WHO'S GOT YOUR SOUP?

Once you have made a proper reservation and selected your table, the stage is set for you to do your part. Remember that you're operating on two fronts: Pacing the lunch and directing the conversation with your client. Don't become intimidated or worried and meekly wait for directions from the restaurant staff. "When you are in a restaurant, the staff should not be the ones to dictate to you what should be done." Jean Pierre Sire says. "*You* should take charge of the staff."

Indeed, restaurant staff members in good business lunch restaurants are trained to take your directions and implement your desires. They accomplish this unobtrusively, in a polished, professional manner. "We teach our staff to take the fear away from the host so that he can pay attention to business," Nick Nicholas says. "We don't want the host to worry that 'these guys are going to mess up, which is going to mess up my lunch, which is going to mess up my business deal.' We are trained *not* to mess up, and we don't make many mistakes."

Since you have the responsibility of running the lunch, you must feel comfortable in communicating with the maitre d' and in directing the captains and waiters. But how do you work with these allies?

Let's review some basics. The chain of command in the typical business lunch restaurant consists of several teams of waiters and busboys, each commanded by a captain. The captain will probably be dressed in a different uniform than the waiters — usually a black jacket and tie but, in all cases, dressier than the waiters. Your captain will greet you, take your drink order, give you menus and take your food order. From then on, the waiter, frequently wearing red although it could be any color, will serve you. The busboy, in white or brown, will clear your table, fill your water glasses and serve you coffee.

In some restaurants with a more complex structure, there also is a front waiter, a back waiter and a runner. The runner brings the food from the kitchen, and the back waiter is responsible for the front waiter's needs. But generally, the structure is: Maitre d', captain, waiter, busboy.

After the maitre d', the next most important staff member for you to know is the captain. That's because he will be responsible for the area in which you are sitting and he's the catalyst for much of what will happen with your service. To communicate effectively, you've got to establish a relationship with him.

The reason you must establish a businesslike relationship with the captain is that he and the waiter have several tables to handle. If you have forged a special relationship with him, he will try harder to please you.

One way of doing this, according to restaurateur Sinclair, is by saying when you greet him: "We're looking forward to a very pleasant lunch here this afternoon, and I've heard that you're one of the outstanding captains!" That sets up your relationship, and although the captain usually will be startled, he will try like hell to live up to his "reputation."

We've all had waiters and captains who seem mentally detached when they are taking menu selections. Sinclair recalls one such experience when his waiter was paying more attention to the legs of the woman at the next table than to his guest's order. "I actually reached out and touched his arm just to bring his attention back to our table," Sinclair recalls, "And I said, 'We're really looking forward to having lunch here.' Suddenly, I got him."

Conversely, it's important not to establish an adversary relationship. If you sit down at a table and your first communication to your waiter or captain is a complaint about a dirty fork or spotted glass, you have already initiated an antagonistic relationship that's damaging to a power lunch. Since you are already critical of him, you will not have his commitment to your team effort.

A fictional executive we'll call George Williams is a fairly successful seat belt manufacturer who invited the buyer (Bill) from a major auto company to lunch at the

London Chop House. Williams is used to flaunting money, and he tips the doorman and maitre d' with gaudy flourish in full view of Bill. When both are seated at the table, George bellows to the captain, "Hey! Nothing but the best for Bill! If you find some of that three-pound lobster that isn't on the menu, there's another ten in it for you."

George believes that the phrase "money is power" means the more openly he displays his wealth, the more successful he will be. He doesn't realize his bullying, ostentatious behavior actually demeans the staff and humiliates his guest. In reality, George's hot air has melted his power.

Once you're on proper terms with the maitre d' and captain, what is the proper way to summon them? Look up, catch their eye and say, "Sir!" or "maitre d'!" if you don't know their name. Do not — *DO NOT* — snap your fingers, clap your hands, whistle or shout, "Hey you!" or "Boy!" In a high-caliber restaurant, you should always be able to communicate with the staff in a consistently polite manner.

Even with the most professional restaurant staff, though, mistakes can occur. How do you communicate when something goes wrong at a power lunch? Most experts agree a power lunch is not the right place to critique the food. So unless there is something so seriously wrong with your dish that it's inedible, you should eat it and proceed with your lunch. If your guest has a complaint, however, politely and promptly summon the captain, who almost always will remedy the situation. If there is a service problem or a serious oversight, then you must relay it to the staff. But don't do it in front of the guest. Excuse yourself and speak discreetly to the maitre d'.

Don't follow the example of our friend George who, when Bob's steak arrived and it was not prepared according to his request, played the overbearing host and said: "Hey, Dennis, what's goin' on with you guys? I bring in my top client and you serve him bum meat!" Needless to say, even if Bob has not actually left the table by this time, George has certainly been "knighted" a wimp.

Remember that the more *sophisticated* the power luncher, the more *subtle* he is. He's always able to settle any problem with the least possible fuss and interruption.

In most high-quality power lunch restaurants, if you have given the maitre d' enough input and are a frequent customer, everything usually will go smoothly. And the more you lunch, the more expert you will become. Just remember the restaurateurs and their staffs are eager to help you.

As Nick Nicholas puts it, "At a business lunch, we want you only to worry about business. If the host spends half the time doing business and half the time looking for the waiter, that's when he blows it!"

Choosing the Power Seat

Jockeying for Position

7

Each day, millions of business lunchers and their guests arrive at restaurants across the country and are seated at tables next to service islands, across from restrooms or beside kitchen doors. Embarrassed by their lack of influence but reluctant to complain in front of their guests, the hosts usually accept the offered crumb of a table. And even before the lunch has started, they feel defeated without really knowing why.

The reason they land such lousy locations is that they have stumbled into power lunch restaurants where the power pecking order of the regulars is so intense that status tables can be more sought-after than awards, lovers or mistresses. Unless you are a power luncher, you're unaware of the competition and consequently out of the game.

"At least 20 percent of our tables are occupied by the same people every day," says Tom Margittai of New York's Four Seasons restaurant. "And the more frequent customers move up to the best tables." Not only are these regulars guaranteed their own tables, but also their own seats. "If a guest arrives earlier than the host of the regular table and by mistake takes the host's seat, we diplomatically ask him to move because the host couldn't, of course, do so," Margitai says.

So if you want to become a power luncher, it's imperative you learn which are the prime areas and power tables of the restaurants you frequent — and how to obtain them.

"There's no question about it," a prominent real estate and hotel tycoon said when asked about the unspoken pecking orders of various leading restaurants. "For instance, at Chasen's (in Los Angeles), the place to be is on the left as you come in, in the first small room. In Le Cirque (in New York), the prime spots are along the right wall as you enter. That's where, as Women's Wear Daily puts it, you can see the same people every day, 'the rich, the beautiful, the famous.' In Chicago's Ciel Bleu, everyone wants a window table, and at Cricket's, the choice seats are the corner tables in the first section."

Restauranteur Nick Nickolas concurs. "Our regular customers know our tables by number. When reserving, they ask for Number 12 or Number 17, for instance. They know the numbers of the tables in the front, where they want to show off, and those in the back, if they want to hide."

The idea is to learn the lay of the land: Which are the power tables to strive for. "A restaurant is not only for dining," as Arturo Petterino puts it. "You are assuming your place in a stage setting." And most power lunchers know the most powerful tables usually are the ones closest to the maitre d' and, of course, far from sidestands, lavatories and kitchen doors.

HOW TO GET OUT OF 'SIBERIA'

As explained earlier, to become a power luncher you must (1) visit restaurants where you are known and (2) lunch out frequently.

It's difficult to believe how many people have business lunches almost daily but never think of the restaurant as a main arena of business life. So they haven't taken the time to become acquainted with the seating structure in top restaurants, much less made an attempt to win an influential spot. With all the other power lunchers vying for tables, it's not surprising that those who are unaware of the backstage competition are placed in what is frequently called "Siberia." That's the least desirable area typically reserved for first-timers, out-of-towners without influence, parties in polyester or family groups.

"Everyone wants the same tables — the best ones in the house," says Jean Pierre Sire of Chez Paul. "No one calls and asks for 'just a little table by the kitchen.' It's always difficult for the customer who comes in for the first time to get the best table. If someone I've never seen before tells me that this is an important lunch and he wants the table where I usually seat Phil Donahue, I will say most of the time, 'No, I can't give it to you; I already have someone for it.'"

The question, then, is how to work yourself up to the power tables. The answer: Visit the restaurant frequently.

One restaurateur has even formed a private club for his most frequent customers. Jovan Trboyevic, owner of the internationally renowned Le Perroquet restaurant, frequently cited as one of the country's top dining establishments, often is asked how someone can join this very exclusive society, called Les Nomades. Jovan's answer: "Come to Perroquet at least three times a week, if not every day, and you will receive a membership card."

Nearly everyone agrees that the V.I.P. spots go to diners who visit often. Jean Pierre Sire summed it up this way: "How do you get the window table? If I see you here about three times per week for two years, you will get the window table. You have to work up to it."

As a last resort, though restaurateurs and their staffs are reluctant to discuss it, you might be able to secure a prime table by including an appropriate amount of cash in your handshake with the maitre d'.

THE POWER CHAIR

How often have you, as a typical business luncher, met your guest at a restaurant, possibly slipped the maitre d' a gratuity to obtain a better table than your lack of frequent patronage warrants, and then sat down to discover: (1) You can't see your guest because the sunlight is glaring into your eyes; (2) Your guest, sitting across from you, seems a block away because you're at a deuce turned sideways; or (3) You find yourself sitting side-by-side at a banquette with a guest who, you suddenly remember with horror, has a bisexual reputation.

Every power luncher knows that getting the best table is only the beginning. Next comes an equally important test: Selecting the power seat, the spot that gives you the greatest advantage and eye contact with your guest, while at the same time making your guest feel comfortable and complimented.

WHOSE BACK IS TO THE WALL?

Let's start with the power seating problem involving two diners because this will be the most common dilemma you'll face. Usually a deuce, as a table for two is called in restaurant parlance, has one seat against the wall, perhaps a banquette, and a pull chair across from it. Which is the power seat?

Though most casual business lunchers may quickly conclude the seat facing the dining room is the power seat, experts are divided on the point.

It's crucial in choosing the power deuce seat to remember that circumstances change depending on the restaurant and your guest. In each case, you'll be faced with some basic decisions and you must learn to shape your strategy based on each situation. Here are some important points to consider:

If you allow your guest to sit on the banquette facing you and the room, he will have the more favorable view and usually a more comfortable, cushiony seat. But — and this is a big but — his attention could be captured by the room and diverted away from you. Essentially, you are taking the chance that what's going on behind your back may be more intriguing than what you are saying. Also, you will have a more difficult time summoning service because you'll be facing your guest and the wall. The result can be more serious than a sore neck. You can lose the very essence of any power lunch — eye contact.

On the other hand, if you seat your guest on the pull-out chair, and you sit on the banquette facing the room, you are placing yourself in a more obvious power position. You're in command. Your guest is forced to look at you and virtually no one else, yet you can scan the room and summon not only waiters, but important friends who might be impressive to your guest.

"If you want to intimidate the guest, you sit against the wall and wave people over," says one prominent power luncher. "Then the guest is much more confined, and you can pick and choose who you want to wave over."

"Can you give us a table near the 'in' people?"

So your choice often depends on your guest. If you have a guest with a strong personality who can tolerate the facing-the-wall position without feeling intimidated — or if you *want* to intimidate someone — select this seating arrangement. But don't do this with guests who might be too insecure or who you want to pamper. Allow them to sit on the most comfortable seat, facing the room, even though you realize it will be more difficult for you to maintain your power.

A well known Beverly Hills maitre d' feels there are benefits to having you facing the wall and your guest facing the room: "While you're giving orders to the captain, your guest has a chance to enjoy the ambiance of the room." He feels that the opposite seating creates too much tension for the guest, making it difficult for him to relax. Maitre d' Jean Pierre Sire claims that if the host wants to control the service, he should face the dining room so he has eye contact with the staff.

A lobbyist for the oil industry in Washington, D.C. says: "I like to face the door to see who is coming in. I would have the guest sit facing me. If I face the door, I might notice someone I've been trying to see all day.

Another power luncher, a prominent hotel and real estate tycoon, feels he has solved the dilemma. "When it comes to seating, my approach is not power, but trying to be more easy-going and relaxed," he says. "By trying to make people feel more comfortable, I achieve more. The only time I try to intimidate is by innuendo, not directly. There are people who are very successful that way, overwhelming and dominating by sheer force, but I wouldn't be comfortable with that."

Being comfortable is the key word. If you are at ease in forcing your guest to look only at you while you sit with your back against the wall, by all means do it. But if you feel comfortable letting your guest have the prime seat with its subtle benefits, then take that approach.

CELEBRITY SEATING.

An exception to that flexible approach is when you take a celebrity to lunch. Always seat the celebrity facing the wall. That will ensure he isn't disturbed by other diners or autograph-seekers and will allow you to conduct your lunch with relatively few interruptions.

A glaring illustration of poor celebrity seating involved a prominent publicist in Cricket's restaurant in Chicago. A well known television star, the publicist's guest, was seated in the front part of the main dining room in full view of almost everyone in the restaurant. It wasn't surprising that the poor publicist had a difficult time engaging the star's attention, since everyone was waving at her. The publicist probably wanted to show off her guest, but lost all power in the process.

An example of how correct celebrity power seating saved the day was the first time co-author Ligita Dienhart met Herb Caen, the famous San Francisco columnist. As she waited for Caen to arrive for lunch at the Bankers Club atop the Bank of America Building in San Francisco, she was seated at a deuce situated sideways toward the window. Caen, known as Mr. San Francisco, usually stops traffic when he enters any dining room in the city, and this was no exception. When he walked in, the whole restaurant was in a hush, and all eyes were on him as he sat down. Ligita knew she was in trouble. "Mr. Caen," she said immediately, "I would love it if you would sit facing the view so you could point out the sights of San Francisco to me." And she signaled the maitre d' to turn their table appropriately to place Caen facing the window and away from his curious fans. Caen was delighted to talk about his favorite topic, the city he loves, and be given his privacy.

CHOOSING YOUR SEAT ACCORDING TO YOUR HEIGHT.

Your height and your guest's height are other considerations in deciding whether you should choose the banquette or chair. To be in the power position, you should be slightly higher than your guest when seated — but only slightly because he would feel uncomfortable if you were to tower over him. If you're short, you should select the chair instead of the banquette because you can't afford to sink even two inches into the cushion. Again, you have to be familiar with the restaurant. You'll sink further in some seats than others. But remember: The odds are against you if you are a woman or a short man trying to power lunch a guest while seemingly seated a foot below him.

If you are tall and have a shorter guest, you should be careful not to take the higher seat, which usually is the chair.

Another factor to keep in mind when entertaining a tall guest is the proportions of the restaurant so that you can avoid the "bull in a china shop" syndrome. Make sure the tables and chairs are roomy, with plenty of leg room, and the glassware and china are sturdy. We have all seen tall men — and even tall women — uncomfortably squeezed at tables where they can't even cross their legs, and where they are drinking from dainty, thimble-sized wine crystal. A guest won't feel comfortable or complimented when physically ill at ease.

So before deciding too quickly which is the power seat at a deuce, analyze your guest — their personality, how you think they might react under different situations and, above all, what your objectives are with that guest. Then decide which is the power seat for that specific lunch.

THE FOURTOP: 'HE WHO HAS THE CORNER OFFICE ALSO HAS THE CORNER TABLE.'

To avoid the problems of the deuce against the wall, it's best to sit at a table for four — a "fourtop" in restaurant terminology — even if there are just two of you. The chairs will be of equal height and you certainly will have more room at the table. But again, you have to select your power seat. The most powerful fourtop usually is located in a corner near the maitre d', which means there will be two seats with backs against the wall and facing the room. Which do you take?

In traditional etiquette, a guest sits on the host's right. But this usually applies to large tables where many people are seated. In a twosome, power lunchers and leading restaurateurs prefer the guest on the host's left.

"Putting your guest on your left is a little more forceful for you if you're a right-hander because you're eating with your right hand and have a tendency to look to your left rather than to your right," says a New York advertising executive. If you are a smoker, you must definitely have the guest on your left so you avoid holding your cigarette in your guest's face. Even so, Jean Pierre Sire makes the point that "no matter where you are seated, the smoke will always go toward the non-smoker."

If the fourtop is in the middle of the room, most experts advise that you sit adjacent to your guest, not across from him, and with your guest to your left. You should face the maitre d' and be certain your guest's chair is farthest away from any traffic or other annoyances. But some, like the Four Seasons' Tom Margittai, say that even at a fourtop, sitting across from your guest is the better position because it permits better eye contact.

If there are three of you at a fourtop, the host should avoid sitting in the middle because this creates the tennis ball effect as you try speaking with both your guests. Power lunchers prefer having both their guests sit to their left, with the most important of their two guests across from them and leaving the chair at the host's right empty. When there are four at a fourtop, your most important guest usually sits across from you because your conversation will, of course, generally be directed toward him. If he doesn't sit there, your other guests might feel left out.

For groups of more than four, demand a round table, face the room and place your prime guest at your left. Here, you want your guest near you since there would be too much distance to cover if he sat across from you, and you will want to flatter him by having him sit at your side.

A short word about booths. When you're one on one with a client or prospect simply follow the rules set down in this chapter for table seating. However, it is best to avoid booth seating for more than two people. The service is generally not as efficient and the inside position is somewhat claustrophobic. Also, if for some reason someone is forced to leave the table for a moment, this maneuver can become awkward.

Some restaurants, unfortunately, offer a good deal of booth seating. When it comes to power lunching it is best to cross them off your list unless you can be assured of a table instead of a booth or unless you have only one guest.

Seating, like other aspects of your power lunch strategy, is worth careful consideration and planning. Just as your choice of restaurant varies depending on your guest or other particular needs, so will your selection of the power seat.

Chapter Eight

Liquor and the Power Lunch

"Straight up and Hold the Umbrella"

8

"Do as I say," goes the old saw, "not as I do." What does that have to do with power lunching? Plenty — if the topic is as touchy as liquor.

Among our long-time business friends and lunch partners are the advertising vice-president of a world wide food processing corporation and the vice-president in charge of sales for an international airline. Before this book was published, we called them to request a review of our book that we might use for promotional purposes. We told them we wanted to use their name and corporate title.

"Of course we'll do it," was essentially their reply. But when they got to the chapter called "Liquor and the Power Lunch," both regretfully withdrew their support. It's not that they don't consider what and when they drink as important components of power lunches. But they didn't want to put their corporate seals on a book in which one chapter discusses, without disapproval, drinking at a business lunch.

"Do as I say, not as I do."

I'LL DRINK TO THAT.

"I don't drink any more.

"However, I don't drink any less.

"I'll have a triple Beefeater martini on the rocks, hold the ice!"

Many yesterdays ago, that may have been the attitude of

many people on how to start a business lunch. It's wrong! That *was* yesterday; this *is* today.

There's nothing new, of course, with booze — whether it's hard liquor, wine or beer — being used in social and informal business settings. Cavemen fermented, brewed or distilled some type of alcoholic beverage to get a little high, and it's believed they used it during get-togethers with neighbors and people they knew from far away. Wine was served at the Last Supper. There were drinks consumed when we purchased Manhattan Island from the Indians (mainly by the Indians). And the prints we see of elderly, well-to-do gentlemen at their private clubs certainly include cocktails.

Booze may be too crude a word for some of you. "Cocktail" has a more genteel ring. But cocktail, booze, aperitif — the label doesn't matter. What we're talking about is the skillful handling and consuming of liquor at a power lunch.

WELCOME, MY FRIENDS!

The benefit of booze at a business lunch is that it can dissipate tension and help create a friendly, easy-going atmosphere. It also offers an opportunity for a toast: "To your very good health," "Good to see you," "Cheers," "Long life!" In addition, the presence of an alcoholic beverage emphasizes that you're away from the office, and this contributes to the sense of relaxation, trust and sharing. But there's a downside to liquor: Although your guests may enjoy the cocktails, they might be a bit on guard because they know alcohol looseneth the tongue. Because of its potential impact, it's best to use caution and planning when dealing with booze in a business lunch setting.

BELLY UP TO THE BAR?

The bar presents the first opportunity for a drink at a business lunch. Resist it. Whether the bar is luxurious and spacious or is stand-up and three-deep, avoid it unless you're very close to your guests and know they're comfortable there. The bar's drawback is that it permits no opportunity for private conversation. You're going to be jostled, pushed and whatever you say will be very public. Your table is the proper place for the first cocktail or drink.

THIS MUST BE THE PLACE . . .

You and your guests are now seated at your table in the manner discussed in earlier chapters. The waiter or captain approaches and says something like, "Gentlemen, ladies, would you care for something from the bar?" Or, "May I serve you a cocktail?" At this moment, look at your guests individually and say something like, "Ms. Jones, what would you like?" Have her tell you, not the server, what she prefers, and then you should relay that order to the person serving you. Go around the table that way, asking each person what he'd like. A good waiter or captain will hear these orders as they are spoken to you, and usually you won't have to repeat them.

WHATARYA GONNA HAVE, BUDDY?

What should you drink? The possibilities are endless. There's hard liquor — scotch, bourbon, rye, gin, vodka, blends, Irish whiskey, etc. There are mixed drinks — martinis, Manhattans, highballs, for example — that have a hard liquor base plus varying amounts of other ingredients or "mix," such as soda water, ginger ale, plain water or tonic. Don't — please don't — select a fancy drink like a Mai Tai, Devil's Flower or anything served with a paper umbrella or a lot of vegetables or fruit, which are known in the trade as "garbage." One exception: the Bloody Mary. Yes, it does sometimes have a celery stalk, but it's served often over ice cubes in a moderately large, not-too-tall glass.

Two things work to your advantage when drinks are served on the rocks. First, the alcohol becomes somewhat diluted as the ice melts. And second, it's easier to handle and bring to your mouth without the risk of spilling. On the other hand, a drink that's served "up," usually in a stemware glass, is often filled quite close to the top and therefore presents more opportunities for slippage and embarrassment. It also seems no bartender in the world can make a mixed drink that contains anything sweet or syrupy without spilling some onto the stem, giving you sticky fingers.

To display power, order any whiskey — scotch, rye, gin, vodka, you name it — "neat," that is, no ice and no mixers.

Make sure it's served in an on-the-rocks glass, so that you have ease of handling, as "sippin' whiskey", and not in a shot glass. Whiskey is a macho drink and conveys power. But beware that if you drink straight whiskey, which at a modest 86 proof is 43 percent alcohol, you have a better chance of getting bombed than someone who dilutes his drink with a mixer. Mixers also have the advantage of helping you "stretch your drink," which means you consume the beverage over a longer period of time and thus take in the alcohol at a slower rate.

DRAW ONE!

Some haughty people may look down on beer at a business lunch, but actually it's quite appropriate if properly ordered and handled. Virtually any restaurant you choose for your power lunch will have several brews available. The best approach is to order a draft beer, which will be served in one of several types of glasses designed for beer consumption. Ordering beer in a bottle has an unsightly side-effect: No matter how short of a time it sits on your table, the sight of empty bottles is very unattractive. A stein or glass, in sort, projects a better image.

IN VINO VERITAS.

Wine has become a popular substitute for mixed drinks, and is certainly acceptable at a business lunch. But don't make the mistake of believing that by having a glass of wine instead of, say, scotch, you're consuming less alcohol. Drinking a glass of wine can mean you're taking in four, five or six times more beverage than the person who's drinking scotch on the rocks or bourbon and water. Wine may have only a 12 or 14 percent alcohol content, compared to 40 or 50 percent for most whiskeys, but you'll be drinking several times more than the one-and-a-half ounces of alcohol the hard-drink person is consuming. Enjoy your wine or beer before your lunch, but be on guard: The alcoholic content of a full glass of beer or wine is essentially the same as that of a cocktail or highball.

HERE'S TO YA!

The cocktails have been ordered and served. It's an obvious social courtesy not to pick up your drink until all have

"It's a nice wine. Leggy, yes, yet pleasantly full-bodied. Has a unique character. It's vigorous, but not too piquant. God, I'm wasted."

been given theirs. As the power-possessing person who's running the show, it's up to you to slightly raise your glass and propose a modest toast. Look your guests in the eye and offer a simple, "Cheers," "Glad we could get together" or "Nice to see you!" This gives each person an opportunity to establish eye contact and gets the lunch rolling in a friendly, trusting manner.

ANOTHER ROUND?

Cocktails encourage conversation, and as the guests roam from topic to topic, the drinks get lower and lower in their glasses. Soon the waiter, captain or maitre d' asks if anyone would like another round. (If his arrival is tardy, it's up to you to keep tab on how the drinks are progressing and signal for him when he's needed.) At this time, you should pause, look around the table and ask, "Do you care for another drink?" Anyone who says, "Thank you, no," shouldn't be pressured. For those who do want another, place the order with the serving person. Don't become concerned about ordering a drink for yourself even if none of your guests join in. But remember: It's considered out of line to consume more than one drink above the number consumed by any guest at your table. This can do you more harm than good, regardless of how much "power" you're trying to display. One way to proceed if you sense some hesitancy on the part of your guests to order a second round is to say, "Why don't we have another drink and we'll look at the menu at the same time?" This usually works.

LIPS THAT TOUCH LIQUOR . . .

It's not unusual to have a guest reply, "Thank you, but no," when the initial drinks are ordered. This certainly need not embarrass anyone. You might want to ask, "Would you care for something else?" Or, "Would you like coffee or tea at this time?" If the answer is still negative, simply pass. Respect your guest's wishes. No one should feel self-conscious, and it certainly shouldn't preclude you or your other guests from ordering a cocktail. If the situation is reversed — that is, your guests order drinks and you don't want one — there are several options. The easy approach is to simply order club soda and lime or another non-alcoholic beverage. This allows you to hold a glass in your hand as your guests are doing so that you can participate in the warm camaraderie and freedom to speak that characterize cocktail time. Or you can order a very mild drink such as a spritzer, a small amount of (usually) white wine in a tall glass with a large amount of club soda. You also have the option of saying something like, "Doctor's orders; I can't this time." Whatever your choice, keep it simple. Your guests will understand and won't be inhibited.

BRAZEN HUSSY!

Unlike years ago, there's no great distinction today between how men and women handle cocktails at a business lunch. If a lady wants to order a Beefeater martini, so be it. If she asks for a glass of wine or a Campari and soda, that's fine, too. Keep in mind, though, that there are some gentlemen of the "old school" who consider it unladylike for a woman to order a "man's drink." If you're female and believe bowing to this old-fashioned nonsense works to your advantage, then go along by ordering a white wine. Don't order a "lady's drink," such as dry sherry or a Pink Squirrel. That's a hundred yesterdays old and its impotent image will drain your power. You'll gain nothing and lose much.

TWO FROM COLUMN 'A,' NONE FROM COLUMN 'B.'

If you're hosting a power lunch, your choice of drink should convey your dominance. Here's a list of "power drinks:"

   Scotch

   Bourbon

   Gin martini

   Vodka martini

   Any whiskey served "neat" or with a simple mixer

   Club soda

Drinks melting in the "wimp" category include:

   Whiskey sour or any drink with fruit or vegetables

   Perrier

   Coke

Tab

7-Up

Any fancy mixed drink such as a daiquiri or Mai Tai or anything with an umbrella.

DON'T SNIFF THE CORK.

Wine consumption in the United States has rocketed like a runaway champagne cork in recent years. Not only is wine appropriate instead of a cocktail, but it's often a mellow supplement to the meal itself. After the menu has been presented and the meals ordered, you should look at your guests and inquire, "Would you care for wine with your meal?" If there's a uniformly negative response, simply drop the matter. Order a glass for yourself if you'd like.

If they leave the matter up to you, then you have several options. Ask the waiter, captain or maitre d' for the wine list if one isn't at the table (it's unlikely you'll find a wine steward on duty during the lunch hour). Or you can ask your guests if there's a specific type of wine — white, red or rose — that they would prefer. Sometimes, however, you know in advance that one of your guests is knowledgeable about wine. If one of them is, it's a very powerful courtesy to suggest he order wine for the table. He'll be very flattered and you will have brought him closer to you — which builds power points.

Unless you are the consummate wine expert don't attempt to play the "ritual game" with the wine cork or you face the possibility of looking like a wimp. You should simply acknowledge the fact that the waiter has placed the cork in front of you by moving it out of your way. The waiter will accept this signal and pour your wine for tasting. Skip the swirling; simply taste the wine and nod your acceptance. Anything more, unless you are skillful enough to handle it properly, and you risk losing power even before you've had a chance to enjoy your wine.

A final note: One aperitif to avoid, unless your guests are in the restaurant or show business, is Lillet. It's a snob wine, considered very show bizzy and flashy, hardly the image you want to project at a power lunch.

BRANDY MIGHT BE DANDY, BUT A DRUNK IS A DRUNK

So far, everything's proceeding as planned. Cocktails and the meal have been consumed and the conversation has flowed. Dishes have been cleared, coffee or tea has been ordered and the waiter asks, "Do you care for a drink with your coffee?" Unless you need more time at the table with your guests or you get strong vibrations that your guests want an after-dinner drink, it's best to respond with a simple, "Thank you, no." Why? The cocktails have *served their purpose*. You and your guests have become warmer, friendlier, more convivial, more trusting of each other. There's no need for more alcohol, especially because there's the potential for serious problems. Watch the guest who orders one or two drinks beyond what you and the other guests consume. He may think he's having a great time and you're probably happy he's enjoying himself. But there's a chance that when he returns to his office, he's going to be drunk, ill or, at the very least, slowed down to the extent he can't function properly. And remember, he was *your* guest. He may have thought well of you when you were having his glass refilled at the table, but you're the one he'll blame for getting him drunk. He won't regard himself as having had too many drinks; he'll blame *you* for *giving* him too many drinks. Don't let it happen! You will have lost the goodwill you worked so hard to establish.

TO SUM UP

Alcohol and business lunches are certainly no strangers. Properly handled, liquor can contribute to a successful power lunch by relaxing your guests and helping build a trusting atmosphere in which your guests become closer to you. Shy away from fancy mixed drinks, and don't exceed one drink beyond what your guests order. Respect guests who abstain from drinking, and don't worry about losing their respect if you don't join them in ordering a cocktail. It's best, though, to hold some kind of beverage to keep from inhibiting your guests. Keep in mind that a glass of wine or beer has about the same intoxicating impact as smaller whiskey drinks. If enough guests want wine with their meal, you have the opportunity to order a simple wine by the bottle, such as a house wine, or letting a wine-knowledgeable guest display his expertise. Whenever possible, though, avoid after-dinner drinks; they're usually too much and too time-consuming. And most important, don't let your guests over-drink; in the end, you'll get blamed.

To your very good health — and your next power lunch!

Chapter Nine

The Menu and the Meal

You Are What You Order

9

Duck with raspberry sauce? Double sirloin, rare and Caesar salad? Quiche Lorraine and consomme? Spinach salad with bean sprouts?

At a routine business lunch, you probably would just look at the menu and order what you feel like eating. Not so at a power lunch, where your motivation isn't taste but a hunger for success.

So at a power lunch, don't organize the meal around what you would like to see on your plate or what would please your palate. Instead, focus on how the food and drinks you order can best enhance your power image, maintain your control and help avoid distracting you from the business of the power lunch. In addition, you must "time" the meal to best accomplish your purposes.

TIMING IS EVERYTHING.

Harry leans forward and, looking client Frank squarely in the eye, says: "Look, Frank, the reason I wanted to see you is . . ."

"Hello, may I tell you about our specials today? For appetizers, we have marinated artichoke hearts, creamed frog legs and cold cucumber soup. Our entrees . . ."

Or:

While both are eating, Frank asks Harry, "Tell me again why you and your company would do a better job for us than Zinco?"

"Well, first of all . . . Hey, I can't really cut these ribs.

107

Waiter? Can I please have another napkin, my hands are full of sauce. Thanks. Sorry, Frank, now where were we?"

These scenarios are typical of the poor timing encountered by business lunchers everywhere who simply sit down, order and trust that things will take care of themselves.

They won't.

Power lunchers know they are the orchestra conductors who have to plan every "movement" of the lunch in advance — the most important direction being the meal's timing.

Unless your guest indicates when you invite him or when he meets you at the restaurant that he will be very pressed for time, assume you will have between 90 minutes and two hours for your power lunch. When you enter the restaurant (before your guest has arrived, of course), instruct the maitre d' how you want the timing of the luncheon to proceed. By this time, you have researched your guest enough to know if he will have a drink or two or if you will have to order right away.

Now let's go back to Frank and Harry to see what Harry can do to have more control over the lunch — and, consequently, over his client.

Because it's a power lunch, Harry has researched Frank and knows he drinks martinis — usually two — and likes to get the business part of the lunch out of the way before eating. Harry probably will instruct the maitre d' like this: "When my guest arrives, please take our drink order right away and then leave us alone for 30 minutes, except to check for a possible second round. Then, when I signal, please have the captain bring the menus. Also, please omit any recitation of the specials, and simply leave the written menu on our table."

Now Harry is in charge of the lunch. He knows he will have 30 uninterrupted minutes with Frank to talk business, and the staff will watch for *his* signal. He also has eliminated the tiresome recitation of specials which, though rarely practiced in power lunch restaurants, can easily be avoided through advance instructions. Again, you should be familiar with the restaurant to know if it's a place where waiters do describe the specials verbally.

Whether your guest prefers talking business over drinks or, as is more customary, after the meal, a power lunch

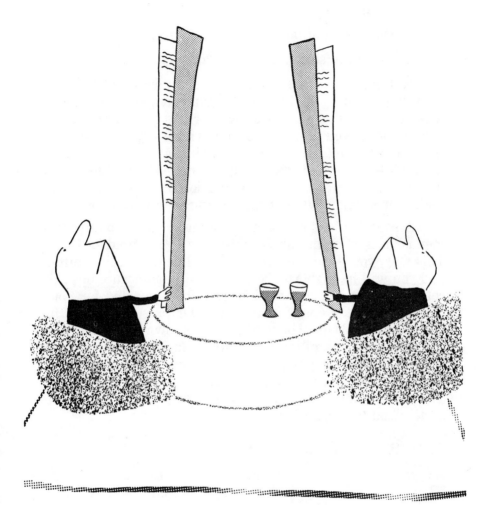

usually follows this format:

1. Drinks (get acquainted, small talk).

2. Meal.

3. Discussion of business (perhaps over coffee).

4. Wrap-up (summary, check and tipping).

Naturally, this is flexible and each power lunch varies slightly depending on the guest, restaurant and situation. But whether you discuss business over drinks or over coffee, it's important for you to know this in advance so you can inform the staff *when to leave you alone.* It's just as annoying to be in the middle of a wonderful pitch during coffee and to have a waiter arrive with a dessert recitation as it is to have him recite the specials while you're trying to have drinks.

A sound rule is to instruct the maitre d' not to give you menus, dessert menus or the check until *you* signal for them. This way, you — not the staff — establish the meal's timing, and you will have short-circuited possible interruptions. (Of course, in top restaurants like the place selected for your power lunch, the check is almost never presented until the host asks for it.) Once you become well-known in a restaurant, the staff will be familiar with your timing requirements and it won't be necessary to give full instructions to the maitre d' each time. But again, power lunchers leave nothing to chance. The safest route is to make certain your intentions are well-understood by the staff.

ORDERING DRINKS.

As you are seated, the maitre d' or captain will say, "Gentlemen, would you like something from the bar?"

At this point, quickly say to your guest, "What would you like?" Or, "What would you care for?" This forces your guest's hand and, if you want to flatter him, follow his lead. Martini? "Make it two, please." Glenfiddich on the rocks? "Make mine the same, waiter." A glass of wine? "Why don't we share a bottle?" Or order what you prefer, as long as it's a power drink. Those *not* in the power drink category are those with fruit, straws, umbrellas, cute names or snob drinks such as lillet. Finally, if your guest orders a club soda, you have the option of ordering one alcoholic drink, but only one. Don't order a Perrier or another fancy water. Pretentiousness always saps power.

Whatever you like, keep it simple (vodka on the rocks, scotch and soda, gin and tonic, etc.); keep it honest (soda instead of Perrier); and, most important, be decisive. No power luncher ever agonizes, especially out loud. "Oh, what shall I have?" I really would like a martini, but it makes me so tired in the afternoon!" Or: "I really need a drink, it's been a hell of a morning." No one cares. Order quickly, don't give your reasons and then get down to business.

ORDER FOR SUCCESS!

The waiter takes the following order from a table of business lunchers:

Barbequed ribs.

Boullabaisse.

Steak sandwich.

Pasta Primavera.

Hamburger plate

Who has ordered the power lunch?

Not the person who selected the barbequed ribs. They will have to use their fingers in eating them, which will get their hands full of sauce, and in some cases will even be "bibbed" by the waiter. Have you ever seen an adult with a bib around their neck and sauce on their hands maintain their power? Maybe at the family picnic — not at the power lunch!

Not the person choosing the boullabaisse, even though they thought they were ordering a more sophisticated dish. They may not get as messy as the barbequed ribs person, but dipping in their tureen for all the different pieces of fish will keep them too busy and distracted to pay attention to the conversation, much less steer it.

The person with the Pasta Primavera won't have the bib, mess or "fishing" problems of his other two companions. But they lose simply because they have ordered a wimp dish. Here's why: Unless you are such an expert pasta eater that you can deftly twine every bite by using the spoon and then pop the neat ball into your mouth, pasta is out as a power lunch food. Most inexperienced pasta eaters spend their time trying to keep the ends of the pasta from slipping from their forks. No one will ever have confidence in a person who can't even manage to get pasta into his mouth.

That leaves the steak sandwich and the hamburger. Both are good power lunch choices, but it all depends on how the hamburger person eats their selection. If they pick it up in their hands and the tomato slips out as they bite, the steak sandwich man is the winner. But if the hamburger person is a power luncher, they will eat their sandwich neatly, with a knife and fork, to avoid a possible mess.

In short, when you select your power lunch meal, you must think ahead about how difficult it will be to eat, how you will look while eating it and whether this is a dish you want to be associated with and remembered for. Often, a power lunch is a first meeting, and what you order will subconsciously leave an impression of you on your guest's mind. Expert power lunchers would rather be remembered for swordfish steak than spinach with bean sprouts. By sushi rather than Welsh rarebit.

There's a good reason why Americans are known for preferring steak, and why there's an abundance of successful steakhouses in the business community. Some restaurants even specialize in presenting steak by the ounce, boasting of how large their servings are. Steak is macho, and the bigger the steak, the more macho it becomes. (Macho here means powerful and, therefore, is applicable to women as well.) Another reason why good steak was one of the first foods identified with power: It's usually easy to eat. That means a business conversation can proceed while the lunchers are taking bites of their "so-tender-you-can-cut-it-with-a-fork" meal.

The explosion of French and American gourmet restaurants, the increased interest in home nouvelle cuisine and the new concern with health and diet have all reduced the importance of steak as the all-time American power food. But, unconsciously, the macho power of steak still influences what are considered power lunch foods. Thus, veal *steak*, salmon *steak* and liver *steak* have a subconscious power advantage over veal scallopini, salmon mousse or chopped liver pate.

Also in keeping with the power image are foods associated with virility, such as raw oysters, or those that appear daring, such as raw meat and raw onions. Foods associated with dairy products, however, connote childhood and usually make poor power lunch foods. These include all cream soups, creamed turkey and chicken dishes.

This is why steak tartare is such a favorite among power lunchers — it's a steak, it's daring (like raw meat and raw onions), it's exceedingly easy to eat and it's honest.

The fact that they are pretentious instead of honest is why so many fancy dishes find themselves on the wimp list. "Do you really want to be eating partridge with gooseberry sauce while you're discussing a corporate takeover?" asks one power luncher.

A typical wimp lunch consists of avocado or coleslaw, consomme, fried chicken and ice cream. A power lunch, on the other hand, might include black bean soup, rare sirloin, sliced tomato and onion salad, and goat or brie cheese (if you must have dessert).

"You're going to be doing a lot of talking," says a New York advertising executive. "Don't order food that means work, like chicken, which requires a lot of surgery. Avoid ribs unless you're in a special rib place. Pick something simple that is very easy to handle so that you can do a lot of talking without fumbling."

Finally, you must match your order to your guest's. If he orders an appetizer, soup and entree, you should do the same and not just "have a salad." The only time you can get away with ordering just a salad is if you're a celebrity, and even then you might cause a stir, as food and wine expert Robert Balzer recalls:

"This was at the Beverly Hills Hotel in 1950, and Gloria Swanson had just finished "Sunset Boulevard." She was as glamorous as she's ever been in her whole life. And the whole room would turn to look at her whenever she would make an entrance because she was ... a star of stars. As we sat down for a luncheon in the Rodeo Room, she ordered, as was her wont, a mixed green salad instead of roast beef or any of the other things on the menu. This was her entree, so the kitchen, the waiter and everyone else felt that inasmuch as this was to be the main course, it should be a large one. So they brought her a large plate — a bale of chopped lettuce and whatnot, very beautifully garnished — but nevertheless in copious quantities.

"She looked at the waiter and said, 'Don't let the teeth fool you; I'm not a horse.'"

At a modern power lunch, you don't need to eat everything on your plate — or even half — if you're on a diet or not very hungry. But order it you must.

KNIVES, FORKS AND DINNER MANNERS

"Manners! What a pleasure it is to see a person who has table manners! It's a lost art. They eat like cattle now," says a well known Italian maitre d', now working in San Francisco.

Is he right? When was the last time you thought about manners — when your mother told you to keep your elbows off the table, or when you admonished your son not to talk with his mouth full of food?

Power lunchers are aware of table manners *all the time* because this is another avenue for them to show their knowledge and sophistication. Let's review ten basics:

1. Power lunchers do not eat anything with their hands, except bread. Using a knife and fork on hamburger and sandwiches gives a much neater appearance and minimizes the chance of accidents.

2. Take small bites, and chew and swallow before speaking or taking a drink. "I think one who eats with restraint begins to take control of a situation," says a New York City maitre d'.

3. Keep your bread or roll on the plate, not in the air, while breaking and buttering it.

4. Silverware, once used, should never touch the tablecloth. Teaspoons remain in saucers and knives are placed across the edges of plates.

5. Never light a cigarette while there is food on the table and, when putting it out, extinguish it *completely*.

6. Dunking bread in sauces might be okay at home or the local Italian bistro, but not at a power lunch. Only the knife and fork are used to pick up food. The bread remains on your bread plate, where it is broken (not cut) and buttered before being eaten in small pieces.

7. Don't drink hard liquor with your meal. Restaurateur Gordon Sinclair points this out as one of the most boorish habits among unknowledgeable lunchers. If you have had a martini or a scotch and soda before lunch, finish it and have wine, tea or water with your meal.

8. The same goes with coffee. Only amateur lunchers have coffee with their meal, coffee shop style.

9. Dab your mouth with your napkin *each* time before drinking wine or water so that the glass remains spotless.

10. Women should wear as little lipstick as possible to avoid getting globs of it on their napkins and glasses. And applying lipstick at the table is another no-no. "I've seen women putting on their lipstick at the table, and then using *my napkin* to blot it. I've even seen them use tablecloths," says one aghast maitre d'.

ZIG-ZAG

Finally, the knife and fork. There are two ways of holding these utensils. There's the continental way, in which the fork remains in the left hand and the knife in the right throughout the meal. And there's the American "zig-zag" way, in which the food is cut while holding the knife in the right hand and the fork in the left, and then the knife is laid down and the fork is picked up in the right to deliver food to mouth.

Since the United States is the only country in the western world where this knife and fork changing takes place, it would be interesting to know how the rather awkward custom originated. In questioning experts, however, we came up with only speculation, such as the theory put forth by Michel Cancellier, Marketing Director for Kobrand, a major wine importer: "This practice started during the frontier days in America where, while the right hand was on the fork, the left was on the gun!"

In fact, the zig-zag fashion of changing silverware is so peculiarly American that, according to one account, it even played a role in world War II military intrigue. Supposedly, four American soldiers were being hidden by a French family after the German invasion of a French village. The German commander was certain, however, that the Americans would be easy to locate. He told his men to simply walk past all the houses at dinner and listen for the clatter of silverware caused by the changing of knives and forks. Then they'd have the Americans!

Since the zig-zag style is not only noisy but awkward, most power lunchers prefer the continental approach. "I think that you're much better off using European table manners," says a Washington, D.C., executive. "And you're much more apt to impress your guest in a most subtle way. If your guest uses the same, he will recognize your sophistication, and if he eats American style, he will still notice that there is a neatness about your style of eating. He will think, 'There is something different about this person' without your having to say anything."

According to many "maitre's d" who were interviewed, you must always remember to hold your fork properly. While the fork is in your left hand, the end of the handle is resting under your palm, and your index finger is extended over the handle for leverage. Never hold the fork in your fist (with the thumb up, baseball style) or under the palm using the thumb for leverage. If your meat is so tough as to require unusual handling of the utensils, call the captain and ask for a sharper steak knife.

Just how far do you go in table manners to avoid offending your guest? It depends on the guest and situation. Sometimes quite far, as this story illustrates:

An American executive was entertaining five business-men at a New York luncheon spot, where the guest of honor was Japanese. All ordered whole artichokes. When they were served, the guest of honor picked up his knife and fork and started cutting into the artichoke and eating the wedges as one would eat head lettuce. The host, eager to save face for his Japanese guest, swiftly followed suit, and the other guests caught the drift and had no choice but to join in. So the maitre d' observed a table of five men earnestly sawing away at the tough artichoke. But the guest's self-esteem was left intact!

WHEN TO LEAVE THE TABLE.

If possible, never until the meal's end.

As in a business meeting, you should be at the table for a power lunch from the beginning until the meal is over to prevent interruptions and maintain momentum. To avoid an obvious problem, visit the restroom before your guest arrives. There are, though, other possible interruptions, such as telephone calls, that aren't as easily avoided.

If you must leave, do so immediately *after* you have finished a course, and preferably after the entree. To leave in the middle of a course is simply being rude to your guest. Leaving after, say, the salad will screw up the service of the next courses and could impair the proper temperature of the rest of the meal. If you must leave temporarily, excuse yourself, place your napkin to the *left* of your plate and get up. At the end of the meal, when you are leaving for good, the napkin should be loosely folded and placed to the left or above the plate — never on top of it.

When you have finished with your entree, place the knife and fork side by side, resting securely in the center of the plate. This is a signal to the busboy that you are finished and will make it easier for him to clear the table.

SET MENU.

One way to control and streamline a meal if you're entertaining more than four guests is to arrange for a set menu. This is recommended in serious power lunches where time might be limited. By arranging the menu in advance, you dispense with taking time for your guest to examine the menu, decide and give his order. After consulting with the maitre d', choose a simple power menu such as clam chowder, New York strip steak, tomato and onion salad and coffee. What you lose in flattering your guests by allowing them to select according to their wishes, you gain in efficiency. The lunch will be served quickly, it will be easy to eat and you will be able to concentrate fully on business.

YOU ARE WHAT YOU ORDER

Most psychologists agree that nonverbal communication makes as definite an impression as anything that is spoken. Because what you order and how you will eat, in a nonverbal way, leaves such an enormous impression on your guest, expert power lunchers have learned to use this nonverbal communication to their advantage. Power lunchers order foods that make them look powerful, daring and decisive. They order dishes that give them an air of competence and agility. And power lunchers are so skilled at graceful table manners that they exude a sense of confidence and control — almost like a concert pianist playing a perfect Chopin etude while directing a skillful business conversation.

Getting Down to Business

Beware the Dog and Pony

10

After a pleasant dinner, they stepped together from the elevator as it opened on the 38th floor. The couple approached the door to his apartment, a scant twenty yards away. Entering, he flicked a switch that filled the room with soft light.

Passing through a wide arch into the walnut-paneled library, he signaled his guest to sit on the tufted, red leather couch. Then he seated himself next to her. A small orange flame jumped from his gold Dunhill lighter. He had time for just one deep drag on his cigarette before he felt the touch of a hand against the short hairs on the back of his neck.

He snapped his head in her direction and screamed: "Enough of this love-making. Let's f__k!"

Getting down to business at a power lunch can include the signing of agreements or contracts, the initiation of serious talks or merely the beginning of initial conversations that will lead to future power lunches. But never forget: Business is the *only* business of a power lunch. And when it comes time to getting down to business, you'd better act with proper control and timing. As you can see from this chapter's opening, some handle those two skills better than others!

Up until now, you've gone through all the foreplay — learning the whys, whos, hows, wheres, whens, whats and ifs of power lunching. Unless you look at a business lunch as a social event, with no need to profit from it immediately or in the future, or unless you're in a charitable mood, there will come a time to get to the business reasons for your meeting.

No matter how many people are sitting across from you at the table, they, too, are aware you aren't the all-time great altruist. They know they have something you want or that you have something you want them to have — at a healthy profit to you. That, not lobster or pasta, is the real meat and potatoes of a power lunch.

Perhaps matters have progressed according to your plans, and you never broached the true business purpose of the meeting during drinks, appetizers or the entree. But with the table cleared and coffee served, *now* is the time to lean slowly forward, speak softly and say, "Gentlemen, let's talk a little business." You'll get the full attention of those at the table for several reasons:

1. Your guest has a sincere interest in hearing what you wish to discuss. He may or may not agree with what you say, but he will hear you out. Unless you choose the mooch of all mooches, he will want to hear your proposal — if only to argue against it.

2. The power lunch, when managed and arranged as outlined, has put your client or prospect in a better frame of mind toward you than before he entered the restaurant. He really enjoyed the lunch, the drinks and the conversation. He feels pretty good, and he has a sense of obligation to listen to you.

3. Like any good general on the buyer-seller battleground, he understands the wisdom of occasionally breaking bread with the enemy to see what he can discover. He probably figures your tongue will be a little looser after a few martinis. Though he's your guest, he may have read this book before you did!

BEWARE THE DOG AND PONY

Whatever the reason, *now* is the right time to discuss business. But don't spoil it by reaching for your four-inch attache case, opening it on the table and withdrawing your calculator, ballpoint pen, legal pad, catalogue and enough copies of a four-color presentation for everyone at the table. That's exactly the type of straw that can break the strongest camel's back. The power lunch table is the time and place to *talk* business, not put on a "dog and pony act."

Sure, it's permissible to have a few papers in a slim leather envelope to refer to or pass around, but not the whole contents of your overstuffed briefcase. That's an easy way to blow a few hundred bucks, a couple of hours of everyone's valuable time, and the esteem you managed to build until you "presented your case" — attache case, that is!

If you truly need a lot of backup material to get down to business, arrange in advance to have the maitre d' approach your table after coffee has been ordered and say to you, "Mr. Fisher, I've arranged for you and your guests to enjoy your coffee in our coffee room. This way, Mr. Fisher, gentlemen."

It's better if the power lunch doesn't need such a heavy hand, but when the situation demands it, that's how it should be handled.

Assuming it's your plan to discuss business over coffee, you still must be ready in case one of your guests says during the entree, "Mr. Fisher, where is the primary funding coming from for this venture of yours?" This guy wants to get down to business *now*, even while cutting into a piece of delicious beef! If he continues to chew and slice, you stand a good chance of holding him off until coffee with, "Mr. Jones, I want you to have all that information, but why don't we wait until we can put our elbows on the table over some coffee?" You've got much better field position if your guest isn't partially occupied with fork, knife, slicing, buttering, chewing and swallowing. *You* want *all* of his attention, and a sip of coffee takes little away from you.

However, if he crosses his knife and fork on his dinner plate and leans back in a waiting posture. GO FOR IT! He's ready to listen, and you'd better be ready to talk. Lean forward slowly, speak softly and give him what you brought him there for — "the business."

Sometimes, particularly when the meeting consists of more than two or three people, the camaraderie of the meal, the comfortable restaurant, the potent drinks and the relaxed conversation take on a life of their own, and the "small talk" rolls like a snowball down a snowy hill. A simple reminder is needed to pull the group back to the reality of why you called the meeting. Keep it simple, something like: "Gentlemen, it's getting a bit late; may we talk a little business now?"

Another direct approach to initiating the business discussion is to say, "Jack, now's the time to qualify this lunch for the I.R.S." Don't be concerned that you will offend anyone. They know why the meeting was called and will listen to what you have to say because if you've taken the time to plan your power lunch strategy this well, you'd be a fool not to have planned your proposal or presentation with great care, too.

Although it's generally best to hold off the business conversation until the end of the meal, a different yet effective variation of the power lunch can be exercised in the following manner, depending on the circumstances:

"Bill," you say on the phone, "I'm glad you and Jack can join me for lunch on Thursday, That's right, 12:30 at Twenty-One. Just one thing, Bill: Why don't I meet you and Jack at your office at noon? That will give us a few minutes to talk business, and then we can jump in a cab or walk over to Twenty-One. Great! See you at your place at noon. Bye!"

Bill and Jack have opened their office to you for a direct business conversation. And you can bet the three of you will still be talking business as you leave their office.

Make sure, though, you stop the business conversation in the halls and elevator, even if you have to be so blunt as to say, "Hold it just a minute please, Bill." He'll get the picture. We don't discuss business in such places.

And don't talk business in the cab or as you walk to Twenty-One. There are too many potential interruptions over which you have no control before you reach the sanctuary of the restaurant. There are plenty of avenues of social conversation you can introduce during this time, as simple as, "Boy, it's beginning to feel like winter," or, "Where are all the cabs when you really need one?"

An executive we'll call Jim recalled how he made the mistake of continuing to talk business in the taxi. "Things were going so well, I decided to go ahead and make my big play right there in the cab," he said. "I was working my way up to my most important point, laying all the groundwork despite the distractions of traffic, and just when I got to the clincher, the cab lurched to a halt and the cabbie announced. 'Well, here we are. That's $4.40.' I ended up fishing in my pocket for cash, my client started getting out and my whole presentation was ruined."

When you're seated at the table and drinks have been ordered, it's a common courtesy to inject a social remark or two. However, if the business discussion at the office went well, don't drop the advantage. This is the time to pick up the business topic. "Now that we're settled down again," you might say, "let's talk some more about your new R&D project." As much as some people may object, and though some find it socially inept, you *can* talk between mouthfuls of food, and so can your guests. *You* may want to use your knife and fork a little less, to listen better and speak more easily, but if your guest wants to talk business *and* eat, don't let him down!

When you get down to business is important, but far more important than the time is that you are *in control* of the timing — that *you* have made the decision concerning how and when to proceed.

EAR TARTARE?

Even though you know a restaurant well and the maitre d' usually provides you with a choice seat, sometimes outside influences can make business conversation difficult, impossible or unwise. What kind of circumstances?

1. The table next to yours, though sufficiently removed, is occupied by four people who are used to speaking to each other from Alpine peak to Alpine peak. During a thunderstorm. A *loud* thunderstorm. You can't hear what your guest is saying and he can't easily hear you. Wait — not yet!

2. Again, you have the table of your choice, with sufficient distance between your table and others, but you're beginning to think you have just acquired superhuman vision. Must be true, since you can

count every hair on the ear of the clod at the table to your right. That's because he has his ear practically in your mouth. How about "ear tartare?" Wait — not yet.

3. The restaurant is overbooked. The regular maitre d" is off to attend his grandmother's fourteenth funeral, which is taking place at the same time as the Yankee's opener. Every good power lunch table is taken, and you and your guest don't have time to wait for one. You sit side by side on a banquette. Wait — not yet!

Don't be upset, and don't let such obstacles throw you. Remember the bit about the lemon: Squeeze it and you have lemonade. "Mr. Augsburg, tell you what. As you see, this isn't the best situation to talk about our proposition. Let's just take advantage of the moment and *really enjoy* the fine food they serve here. I can recommend the brook trout, the veal is the tenderest in town and the aged beef is outstanding. It would do us both good to take our minds off business for a few minutes. What would you like to drink?"

You've got him!

After the meal, which you've subtly accelerated, you have the option of staying at your table if the Swiss Mountain Legion has left or moving to another table for coffee and business. Quite often, the cocktail lounge is sparsely occupied or empty at this time, and it can provide a private place to exercise the *power* portion of the power lunch.

Any way you slice it, you've got to get to the meat of the meal, and the meat of the meal is business. Slice on and on and on!

Remember these keys:

1. The only business of a power lunch is business.

2. Your guests know this is a business lunch and expect you to discuss business.

3. *You* control the timely introduction of the business subject, unless your guest grabs the bait early. In that case, just lean back and reel him in.

4. Don't try a "dog and pony show" at the table.

5. If all the mechanics of a power lunch start off wrong, enjoy the meal and talk business after lunch ends.

P.S. If you are interested in how the opening scenario ended:

She turned slowly to him, not at all shocked by his gambit, and calmly replied: "I bet you're not very good at power lunching, either."

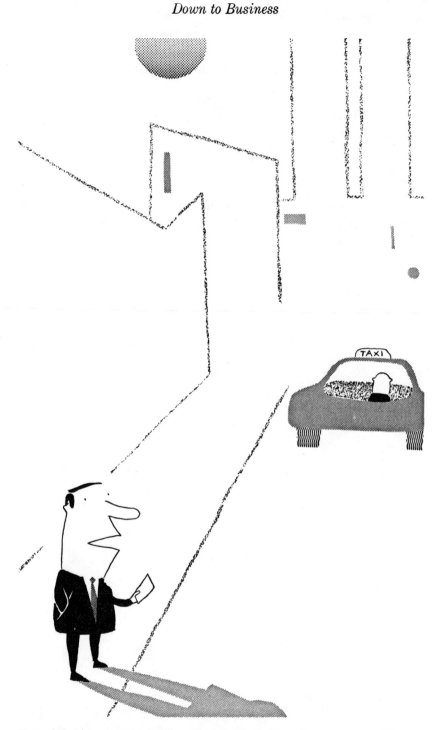

Boy, did I power lunch him. Best table in the place . . . terrific service . . . and Norman Mailer said "Hello" to us! A splendid afternoon . . . I really pulled that one off.

W-what's this? Yow!! I forgot to make my presentation!

Chapter Eleven

The Finale: The Check and the Tip

The End of a Beautiful Relationship

11

Your power lunch is ending. Coffee has been served, dessert has been offered, and now comes the time to pay not only the piper, but the chef and dining room staff as well. After all, didn't they play a key role in making you look good in front of your client?

Now's the time to call for the check to be brought to your table (unless, of course, you have made arrangements with the maitre d' to sign it elsewhere, a tactic that certainly has merit). Top restaurants instruct their staffs never to give a customer his check until he asks for it. In requesting the check, power lunchers should keep it simple. Say merely, "May I have the check, please?" Avoid cutesy phrases that immediately mark you as an amateur, such as, "Hey, Charlie, can I have the bad news?" Or, "Garcon, l'addition, please." Or, "Let's see the damage, please." Often, these boorish remarks are accompanied by the flash of a thick roll of bills.

The check will be placed face down or in a check cover. Say, "excuse me" to your guest, turn a bit away from the table and discreetly examine it. "Today, most addition is done on electronic registers, so there usually is no need to add the check except to see if there are any items included that you didn't order," says restaurateur Gordon Sinclair. "It's not expected that in a fine restaurant they're trying to rip you off by adding something you didn't have. They merely pushed the wrong button and a wrong item came up. A quick glance at the check should satisfy the customer that it's in order."

HOW TO PAY

You can pay the check by credit card, house charge or cash. Contrary to publicity campaigns by major credit card companies, restaurateurs always prefer cash over other forms of payment. The reasons are simple: They save two to six percent charged by the card companies, and cash payments immediately improve their cash flow, whereas a credit card company either pays monthly or the credit must be processed through a bank. So from the restaurant's point of view, cash is still king. And if you become known as a "cash person" in a restaurant, you may receive preferential treatment because the staff also prefers its gratuities in cash rather than receiving tips that have passed through the restaurant's accounting system, making them traceable by the Internal Revenue Service.

DON'T LEAVE HOME WITHOUT IT.

Unfortunately, cash isn't a viable expense-account device for most power lunchers, so usually they pay by credit card. American Express, followed by Diner's Club, have more status than such cards as Visa or Master Charge. It's good advice to carry a second card all the time, especially in a strange city or new restaurant, just in case something goes wrong with your American Express. Indeed, many power lunchers have two American Express cards — a gold and a green, each with different account numbers, just as insurance.

THE HOUSE CHARGE.

Second to cash, most restaurateurs prefer customers use their house charge — but only if they pay their bills promptly. A house charge also is a good image-builder for power lunchers. It can signify that you dine at this particular restaurant frequently and probably are on a first-name basis with the maitre d' or owner. But caution: There's no greater loss of power than a diner eating at a restaurant where his house charge is 90 days overdue.

THE TIP AND THE ONE-TIME POWER LUNCHER.

"I would do away with tipping entirely, if it were up to me,"

says restaurateur Nick Nickolas. "Sometimes, I've spent $60 and I haven't even sat down yet."

In spite of the controversy over the practice of tipping, and the guilt, anxiety and resentment it often evokes in diners, power lunchers know that tipping — and tipping *well* — is essential to obtaining good seating and professional service in top restaurants. After all, just as you wouldn't skimp on your office assistants' salaries, your assistants in a restaurant — the maitre d', captain, waiter and even busboys — are all there to help you and make you look good, so you must award them accordingly.

Even though it may be poor business, you can be sure restaurant staffs prejudge patrons on whether they're apt to be poor tippers, and this undoubtedly influences service. Says Houston restaurateur and consultant Gerard Brach: "The worst thing for a staff is to see a man walk into a restaurant wearing white socks or looking like a doctor — you know your tip is going to be bad. If it's all women, you know your tip is going to be bad. If he smokes a pipe, you know the tip is going to be bad. So it's a very difficult thing for the emotional state of the employees to go through all that. It would perhaps be better if you blindfolded them!"

But there's a flip side to that: Experienced power lunchers, because they go to a restaurant frequently and tip well, are recognized and welcomed by staff members. Says a West Coast sales executive: "You tip more than you should so that when you go back next time, you have the undivided attention of the waiters and maitre d'. The restaurant is a battlefield where you conduct your business, and you want your troops to be with you."

Though the current guidelines for tipping are 15 to 20 percent, regular power lunchers should tip 20 percent. When you add this amount to your check or you charge card slip, it will be divided by the house among the captain, waiter and busboys. "In many restaurants, the tips are pooled," says restaurateur Gordon Sinclair. "If you want to take care of someone exclusively, you should inquire about this practice and then give them your tip accordingly. Write on your check, '$5 to Frank the captain,' or '$5 to Joe the busboy,' for instance. Tipping the busboy is quite proper if he has done an extraordinary act of service for you."

The maitre d' usually receives not less than $5 (and never coins). The easiest way to accomplish this is by a handshake with a $5 bill enclosed as you depart. The tip at the bar also should never be less than a dollar and should never come in the form of change. The same is true for the coatcheck person and doorman — each gets a dollar.

Though you usually won't require the services of a wine steward at lunch, the proper tip when you do is between $10 and $15. You are paying not only for his expertise, but also for making you appear more knowledgeable about wines than you really are, which adds greatly to impressing your guests. He should be tipped in cash at the meal's conclusion, or you can write the amount on the back of the check — whether it's a house charge or a credit card.

If all this is too much for you, or if you want to simplify things, follow Gordon Sinclair's advice. "If I'm having an important function, I usually tell the maitre d' to take care of the check and add 20 percent. I give him a credit card and ask him to send me the receipt." If you do this, however, don't forget to tip the maitre d' *well*. And in the case of all tipping, there's no need to discuss the matter with your guest. Do it quietly and discreetly.

Tipping is one of the most critical subjects for the power luncher to understand and master. For no matter how effective you have been in planning your strategy with restaurant staff members before your lunch, failing to properly reward their efforts through adequate tipping can mean they won't assist you in the same efficient manner next time. The result: You could be turned into a one-time power luncher.

But what do you do when service has been inadequate? "If things have gone wrong, that's not the time to 'kick the dog' in a restaurant by not tipping," says a Washington, D.C., restaurateur. Don't take the approach that you'll feel better by stiffing the waiter.

A successful power luncher will leave 10 percent rather than the minimum 15 percent, and then he'll speak to the maitre d' as he leaves. You might say something like, "I was very disappointed with the service, and I'm sorry I had to reflect that in the 10 percent gratuity. But I'm sure that next time, the service will live up to my expectations of such a fine restaurant." This paints you as a reasonable person who expects good service, and chances are the next time you visit, you'll get the service you deserve. Resist the natural impulse to insult the maitre d' or his staff. It accomplishes nothing but blotting your reputation as a power luncher.

Let's face it: With tipping, as with so many other aspects of our society, money brings results. Sometimes, though, cash accomplishes this feat unintentionally. Once, for example, we were dining in the Grand Hotel Oloffson in Port-au-Prince, Haiti. The beautiful veranda dining room is renowned for its excellent food as well as its very slow service. But on this particular day, we were surprised that the service had seemingly improved 100 percent overnight. Then we noticed the motivating factor: A woman had placed a $100 bill under an ashtray on the table to remind her to get it changed into the national currency. The usually lethargic staff members had spotted the generous "tip" and were moving faster than they had in years!

A power luncher, of course, wouldn't purposefully employ such a tactic. And really, there's no need to. Tipping regularly, generously, discreetly — and preferably in cash — is all that's necessary to guarantee the kind of professional service needed to create an effective power lunch atmosphere.

Sex and the Power Lunch

Dining Thigh to Thigh

12

Power, it's been said, is the ultimate aphrodisiac, even more alluring than wealth, charm or good looks. It even catapulted frumpy Henry Kissinger into the unlikely role of a jet-set sex object during his single days. But does sex have a place at the power lunch?

The answer: An unequivocal "yes!" But our reply to the *next* question — is using sexual awareness as a business tool a *proper* consideration — may be more surprising. The answer, again, is "yes" — although with definite qualifications.

USE IT, BUT CONTROL IT.

Playing up sexual awareness has no place at the serious power lunch unless you can handle it with the same care and consideration you give other aspects of your strategy. Only *you* can decide whether you are able to use this additional tool effectively. Only *you* can judge whether you can carry it off by being charming, imaginative and, most of all, discreet. Only *you* can determine whether this ploy will utlimately work to your advantage or undermine the careful preparations you have made for your power lunch.

We are *not* suggesting a quick martini and a hop into the sack, though it has been known to happen. We *are* suggesting an advantage is an advantage, and there may be times when your *subtle* sexuality can be a positive factor. As long as the tactic doesn't go beyond your control and result in sexual *action* instead of mere sexual awareness, we do suggest you consider this powerful addition to your arsenal of business weapons.

We don't believe it's necessary to tell you how to express your sexual interest in another person. However, it *is* important for us to stress that you proceed cautiously and logically instead of emotionally. Remember, you must adhere to all the previously discussed precepts of power lunching. The sexual aspect of the meeting is only intended to strengthen the closeness between you and your prospect or client.

Some power lunchers know how to use that "extra drink" to their advantage, while others are adept at using their sexuality to their benefit. But here's a warning: Both the "extra drink" and the "touch of sex" carry a risk factor. If you can handle the idea of risk, you can probably handle the opportunity to set "closer" to your guest in a subtle, sexual way.

The power luncher, however, *must* maintain control. As with liquor, failing to handle sexuality with great care can turn the "luncher" into the "lunchee." Keep in mind the only reason sex enters into the power lunch is to bring you closer to your guest. It's relatively easy to let your sexual self take over or, worse yet, to let your guest's sexual attractiveness put him or her in control. When that happens, you've lost your leverage and become a sexual wimp. That could be lots of fun or lots of trouble, but it's guaranteed to be of *no business value* to you. And the business of a power lunch, as we've emphasized before, is business.

Plus, there's another risk you face when using sex to achieve your goals: "What do you do for an encore?"

ME TARZAN, YOU JANE.

Initially, let's talk about the man who sets up a power lunch with a female client or prospect. After that, we'll discuss the reverse.

The man must first brush up on his charm and flirtation techniques — skills that continental men keep in tune but which frequently languish, die or never existed in American businessmen.

Here's the scenario: Bill wants to meet with Mary to convince her that the employee benefit program he sells is a better buy for Mary's company than the program currently being used. He sets up a lunch appointment in the correct manner described in earlier chapters. However, being aware of his sexuality and not ashamed of it, he adds "banquette seating" to his list of requirements for the restaurant, and he requests such seating when he makes his reservations with the maitre d'. The restaurant, then, measures up to all other power lunch criteria, except he and Mary will sit side by side — and possibly thigh by thigh.

You might not be as witty as Noel Coward, but the next best thing is to project an image of being able to laugh at the world and, most important, at yourself. "It's so much nicer to be here with you than playing mogul at the office" is a line many women find irresistible. "If all my vice presidents looked like you, I'd be inspired to communicate better with them and probably double our corporate growth" is another line that's obvious, yet flattering.

To make her feel like the most enchanting person you've ever met, try something like this: "Your voice sounded so scintillating on the phone, I tried visualizing your appearance, and I must say you surpassed all my expectations." Or: How can you — so attractive, charming and intelligent — survive in a corporation where I know the climate is so conservative and suppressive?" Or, the clincher: "Forgive me for staring, but I feel like I'm back 20 (or 10 or 15) years ago. There was a beautiful girl in Brazil (or California or the Bahamas) I fell desperately in love with, and she looked just like you."

If lines aren't your style — and they certainly can fall flat if not delivered in a sincere manner by someone comfortable with using them — you can still be charming by simply acting extremely interested in her. Let her talk about herself: Where she was born, where she grew up, where she attended school. Keep it light — i.e., how did she get those high cheekbones, and wasn't the atmosphere at college stifling for someone so creative — rather than why she disliked her mother or what her shrink thinks about this or that. Or you can talk about books and movies (her favorites). Ask her which heroine she identifies with and why. Ask if she had her choice to be born at another time in history, which century would she choose and why. Both of these can be good for at least half an hour of you, the very interested and charming listener, discussing *her*.

What's more, her answers can also yield useful tidbits about her personality.

Now Bill and Mary are seated side by side at a comfortable banquette in the restaurant of his choice. The drinks arrive and Bill's hand brushes Mary's as they touch glasses in a simple toast. As the conversation continues, Bill's thigh touches hers as he leans to hand her a menu. Mary is certainly aware of what has happened. She knows that a banquette lends itself to physical closeness and that the brushing of hands and the touching of thighs was probably not accidental. So if Mary doesn't quietly move a bit away from Bill on the banquette, Bill can assume she enjoys the sexual attraction she has for him. If Bill has played it right and not come on too strong, this will heighten her interest in him as a successful and powerful businessman and, hopefully, won't start her thinking about his next "move."

Lunch affords many opportunities for flirtatious physical contact, always dangerous but nevertheless effective if handled cautiously:

1. Brush her neck or gently lift her hair as you help her with her coat.

2. The moment she sits down next to you at the banquette, reach for her napkin and spread it on her lap.

3. In lighting her cigarette, if she does not reach for your hand, extend yours to steady *her* hand.

4. When you pass the salt and pepper, don't just place the shakers in front of her. Hold them out to allow your fingers to touch lightly as she reaches for them.

5. When making a toast, skip the usual "cheers" and say something more intimate. For instance, "Here's to Kansas City, which produces the most beautiful and charming women in the world."

Obviously, doing *all* of this might be a little much. To be a charmingly seductive luncher, you must select the moves that suit you and that you can pull off without appearing corny.

One female luncher recalled lunching with a rather ordinary man who was quite boring in many ways, but who had prefected one special technique that worked for him. When wine was served, he lifted his glass, looked deeply into her eyes and made a toast like, "To a lovely lady." After that, he preceded each sip of wine by lifting his glass, looking his guest in the eyes, clinking their glasses and saying softly, "To you."

The result: A feeling of intimacy. The outcome: His dining companion was completely won over.

You'll find that after drinks and a little continued closeness, the balance of the meal will transpire like other power lunches, with both of you feeling a bit freer in your conversation. But remember, it's counterproductive to beat her over the head with sex. You've set the tone — you've brought her closer and possibly thrown her off guard. You're very much in control. When you turn the conversation to business, you should have a more receptive guest. If you have played your cards right, she should not be interested in you sexually, but she should be impressed by you as a *man* as well as a businessman. *That's* an advantage. And that's the name of the game.

Now, let's turn the tables.

YOU TARZAN, ME BO.

It's twice as difficult and dangerous for a woman to enter into sexual repartee at lunch as it is for a man. First, the long-used feminine ploys of vulnerability and defenselessness can't be used if a woman wants to hold her power position. Second, the woman takes a greater risk that she will be forced into the sex-object role instead of maintaining her image as a business woman.

The younger, more inexperienced businesswoman is on thinnest ice in this situation and faces the most peril. It's easier for older and more sophisticated businesswomen to get away with using sexual overtones when lunching with male clients who are younger and in a lower corporate echelon.

The business newcomer is in jeopardy of being viewed as immature and not serious about "getting to the top" in business. On the other hand, the established businesswoman will probably be viewed as simply more self-confident. Ideally, a businesswoman using her sexuality properly won't be viewed by her guest as making a sexual *advance*. Instead, he will view her behavior merely as confirmation that she is a sexy woman who is as confident about her sexuality as she is about her business acumen.

For either the rookie or experienced businesswoman, success means leading your client to believe *he* is the one interpreting your moves as sexual. He must not believe *you* are the instigator. He must think your sexuality is a natural part of your total self-confidence. He must be enthralled by it, and his awareness shouldn't get in the way of his opinion of you as a business person.

Walking a fine line? Yes. Dangerous? Definitely! Again, we repeat. The risks are great. But then, they always are when much gain is at stake.

In this situation, it's Mary, the sales rep for a temporary office service, who's inviting Bill, the office manager of a large company, to lunch. Mary knows how to set up and handle a power lunch, and Bill is a current client of hers. She wants to solidify her company's position with Bill, who is continually being pitched by Mary's competitors.

Here are some suggested remarks effectively used by female executives who have shown through their business success that they know when — and definitely when not — to use the advantage of increased sexual awareness:

"Bill, you're in such great shape. You must work out regularly." Even if he's got a slight paunch, he will be flattered.

"They told me you're the real brains behind the department (or company), and now I know why!"

"You have some fascinating ideas on the industry. Have you ever thought of writing a book?"

These comments, and others like them, are effective ego-builders that women can use to enhance the business lunch.

Mary is now seated beside Bill on a banquette in the restaurant of her choice. Since Mary is in command, she's the one who comments about Bill's attractive necktie. When she reaches to straighten it slightly, Bill knows instinctively that

this move is not in Mary's company sales manual. When she then moves closer to Bill to point out an unusual painting on the far wall, Bill can feel the pressure of Mary's breast on his arm.

In this case, it's Bill who is certainly aware of what is happening. He knows a banquette lunch lends itself to physical closeness, and that the straightening of his tie and the touch of Mary's breast are probably not accidental. So if Bill doesn't move a bit away on the banquette, Mary can assume he enjoys the sexual attraction he has for her.

Other physical tricks suggested by women we interviewed range from placing your hand over his on the table as you're making a point, to removing your shoe under the table, kicking him gently and saying, "Oh, I'm sorry. I think I just lost my shoe!" (For this occasion, you should be wearing a very feminine, three-inch heeled sandal.) Your male client will chivalrously reach down to retrieve your shoe and will probably replace it on your foot.

Was Mary successful at her lunch? The only way to find out would be to interview Bill after he has finished his coffee. It's *his* reaction that counts. Her success lies in *his* interpretation of her moves. If Bill thought Mary was "feeling him out" about a possible affair, she lost.

If he thought her sexuality got in the way of her role as a businesswoman, she lost.

If Bill could no longer concentrate on the business reasons for the lunch, but began fantasizing about putting the moves on *her*, she lost.

But —

— if he found himself admiring her as a total woman — feminine yet strong, in control and aware —

— if he started chastising himself for thinking about how sexy she was when it obviously wasn't her intent to be —

— if his business interest in her intensified because she is now a more fascinating person —

— if he finds himself somewhat off guard because of this new-found closeness to her —

She won!

Let's become asexual for the balance of the chapter. We have seen that male and female executives both can introduce sex into a power lunch, particularly with today's sexual freedom for women. If successful, the person handling the power lunch has brought the guest closer on a personal level. That's good.

But as we said earlier, there are pitfalls. One danger is that your guest may be offended by your sexual introduction. This negative reaction may be displayed at the table. As you begin your presentation after the eating has stopped, you may get an answer that's an obvious stall. And as time goes by, when your prospects of closing the deal grow dimmer and dimmer, you realize your sexual strategy didn't work. Or you might not discover you failed until well after the lunch.

NOT EVERY PLOY WORKS WITH EVERY PERSON

What if your introduction of sexuality is taken to mean much more than you intended? You used sex as a business tool, for example, and he or she took it *very* personally. Who's to say lovers can't do business together?

Moral issues aside, lovers or participants in one-night stands will find it increasingly difficult to hold onto their "buyer-seller" identities for long. More likely, you will quickly *lose* the business that sex helped you to gain if your relationship becomes anything more than casual and brief. Be aware, too, that in your own business community or industry, however large or small, secrets like this are hard to keep. As with liquor, which executives use to their advantage but which many corporations frown upon, sex may be understood by individual members of management but decried by the corporate entity. And the odds are that somehow the word will leak out that you are sleeping with a client or prospect. You may close the deal, but open the door to your own corporate oblivion.

So, what have we?

Power lunching is a studied practice of using control of a

147

business meeting at lunch to gain your business objectives. Like the ambiance of the restaurant, the warmth of a cocktail, the good feeling of breaking bread together and the sharing of interesting conversation, sexuality can be another stimulation that can bring your targeted guest closer to you.

And as we have illustrated, close is good. But *how* close?

That, my friend, is up to you.

Chapter Thirteen

Power After Hours

Lunch vs Dinner Meetings

13

The difference between a power lunch and a power dinner is among other things, three or four hours and $100 or $200 more."

Sure we're concerned with cost, but not if we're convinced the money we spend is actually a wise investment that will contribute to hefty profits later. So don't hesitate to enter into another area of exercising power — the dinner.

First let's explore more of the obvious. The power lunch takes place during business hours, and we're sure most executives feel they put in enough working hours each week. Using some of the same techniques and skills of the power lunch at dinner can extend the hours you have available to build your business. After all, most of us are sufficiently motivated that a few extra hours won't stop us from making an important investment in our future. So let's put that potential negative aside.

Another possible drawback to a dinner meeting is that, unlike the power lunch, its late hours detract from the time you have to spend with your family and friends. Again, though, ambitious people realize that's the price they sometimes have to pay if they hope to garner big profits in the future.

Before going any further, let's clarify one important point. When we're talking about a dinner, we're not referring to what most would call a "presentation dinner." No large number of tables in a banquet hall, with a raised platform for the honored guests. The only business of a power lunch is business. Though occasionally it's less direct in its approach, the same concepts for power lunches hold true for what we'll call power dinners.

Keep this in mind, though: Like a power lunch, the guests you invite know why the invitation has been issued. Because of *business*.

As discussed in earlier chapters, power lunches permit you to control the meeting away from distractions inherent in offices. And the restaurant's atmosphere, food and drink provide an opportunity for socializing. Power dinners go a step or two beyond power lunches by increasing the opportunity for socializing and establishing a closer relationship with your client.

TIME . . . BUT USE IT WISELY

But the power dinner is able to eliminate one of the major enemies you constantly fight at power lunches: Time. Some of the best planned and executed power lunches might have yielded even better results if not for that constant thought in the back of the mind: "I've got to get back to the office soon." At the power dinner, you benefit because time is much less pressing. True, you don't want to keep your guest out so late that it hampers his work the next day. But at least there's no meeting or appointment waiting for him after dinner as there is after lunch.

Power dinners also provide a chance to reap the benefits of something we're all familiar with, but which hasn't been mentioned yet in this book: Entertainment. But beware of some potential liabilities. For example, let's say that out of the goodness of your heart, or because you think it could bring some bucks from your client, you plan to expand the power dinner to include an evening of watching a professional baseball game or the ballet.

Forget it!

During the time you and your guest are seated at the theater or ballpark, you have lost all control. His attention is locked onto professional attention-getters: dancers and ballplayers. You're paying for his attention and others are getting it! Also, that old enemy "time," which has been knifed in the heart by the power dinner, has been brought back to life. "Say, we'd better leave soon," you'll find yourself saying. "The play starts in 30 minutes."

But power dinners do indeed allow you to amplify on another sort of entertainment that's also available at power lunches: Food and drink. Sure, you can eat food and consume beverages at a power lunch, but expedience tells us we must limit their enjoyment to some degree. We're not suggesting a power dinner degenerate into a Henry VIII bone-throwing contest, but the opportunity is there to enjoy food a bit more, perhaps to include a wine you wouldn't order at a power lunch and to have more time to savor the atmosphere of the restaurant itself.

And what about the restaurant? In Chapter Five, we discussed the points necessary to assist you in choosing the best restaurant for a successful, profitable power lunch. Those basics also apply to dinners, but they can be expanded upon. For example:

1. You might choose for a power dinner a restaurant that serves its meals in the French manner, where almost every item is individually prepared or finished at your table. That may be too time-consuming and attention-grabbing for a power lunch, but it's quite possibly that extra elegant touch that will add enjoyment and success to a power dinner.

2. A restaurant that otherwise might be an excellent power lunch site is properly ruled out for that purpose if it's half an hour away from the area where you and your client have offices. But since time isn't as important at the power dinner, you can give it a try for an evening experience.

3. Another restaurant might be crossed off your power lunch list because it's attended at midday by too many business types you might want to avoid while with your client. Good thinking. But you should check those same restaurants as possible power dinner locations. There's a good chance that many businessmen who frequent the restaurant for lunch won't go there for dinner. So have your secretary make your reservations for the evening.

As for the dinner itself, your choices of action are very broad. A restaurant that specializes in giant lobsters and three-pound prime aged sirloins would be out of the question for a power lunch, but it could make a great place for a power dinner. You and your guests have the time and ease of mind to better enjoy such sybaritic opportunities. Another example might be a Japanese restaurant that serves food in a manner that makes the meal not just a gustatory delight, but also a joy of service and attention, a place where time is not measured. (Obviously, you have checked in advance to make sure your guest enjoys Japanese food!)

So a power lunch and power dinner are different mainly in degrees. Yes? Well, maybe.

MAYBE NUMBER 1. In an earlier chapter, we discussed meeting your guest for a power lunch at *your* table in *your* restaurant at *your* chosen time. Or there are the occasions when you may meet briefly beforehand at the office and then go to the restaurant. But the power dinner poses a different set of logistics.

Let's set aside for the moment the geographic differences in dinner-hour choices and agree that a power dinner is called for sometime between 6:30 and 8:30 p.m. If you know your guest is a workhorse every night, then no problem exists. But if your guest conforms to the norm, he'll want to leave the office sometime between 4:30 and 6 p.m. Even in the case of a workhorse, you don't want to take to a power dinner a client who has put in such a long day's work that he won't enjoy the dinner — or be receptive to your business proposals.

So you have three options:

A. Let him stay in the office or go off on his own until the appointed time for your dinner. We won't even begin to mention all the negatives attached to this choice. Just forget it.

B. Meet him an hour or so before the time for dinner at a cocktail lounge *other* than the cocktail area of the restaurant you've chosen for the power dinner.

C. Meet him an hour or so before dinner in the cocktail area of the restaurant chosen for the power dinner.

The best choices: either B or C.

Meeting at a different place for drinks adds variety to the

evening. Of course, you have to give as much attention to selecting this other locale as you will in choosing the restaurant itself. Proximity to one another is of prime importance.

The choice is yours. Play it by gut feeling, but *don't* offer the choice to your guest. Remember, this is a *power* dinner, and all the control must be yours. Have a good time, yet remember the reason you and your guest are there: Business!

MAYBE NUMBER 2. Wives. Husbands. Lovers. Friends.

Blessed are those whose spouse, lover or "friend" is an asset to their business. The power dinner affords you an excellent opportunity to get much, much closer to your client or prospect in a setting that becomes less business-pointed when the "partners" are included.

Some will take exception to the idea of including your social partner in a power dinner. But unless your partner has let you know he or she doesn't want to share your business life, or wouldn't think of "ruining" a fine dinner by sharing it with business associates, you stand to gain by including the partner in your invitation. You get much more intimate with your guest. You learn more. You can control more. Even if your guest declines the invitation on his partner's behalf, you have still gained by offering the invitation.

Logistics, of course, become more complicated when partners are invited to power dinners because they may not live in the same area where you and your guest have offices. But don't despair. Your guest will make the necessary arrangements for his partner, and you make the same for yours. Today, it really doesn't matter whether you or your guest arrive at the agreed-upon starting place with partners in hand. We're all big boys and girls now.

Aside: Your partner isn't joining the power dinner to showcase the diamonds and gold you've lavished on her. Remember, understated is better-stated.

Inviting partners to join the power dinner can be that little added stroke that makes the painting come alive. It's virtually guaranteed that your guest will be appreciative for your consideration and hospitality. What else can the guy do but like you a little more for "sharing" with him? And you'll surely know how to capitalize on his appreciation over coffee or at your next meeting, whether it's in your office or at a power lunch.

Remember that the hour or so before dinner is a fine "in-between" time, a transition period to slip from the tension-riddled office routine to the dinner's mellow pleasures. Permit your guest to make the transition smoothly. If he desires to continue the same conversation at dinner, rest assured your partners will find sufficient subjects of conversation to entertain themselves.

Well, the power dinner has gone as you planned. The cocktail hour was pleasant, relaxing and a good transition. The restaurant pleased your guest, the meal was well-chosen, well-prepared and well-served and your client showed erudition in selecting the dinner wine at your suggestion. The French pastry and coffee have been ordered.

No matter whether you are with only one other person — that is, your client or prospect — or if your table consists of four other couples, NOW is the time to lean slowly forward to the man who counts most and say softly, "Jack, let's talk for a moment about that merger idea."

He'll understand and cooperate. He owes you one. The other persons at the table will sense, simply from the bending of your heads toward each other, exactly what's happening, and they will play the roles assigned to them. Naturally, you will have forewarned your spouse what to expect so that he or she will have no trouble spotting your cue.

There you have the differences between lunch and dinner meetings. You know the characteristics of each and how to make the most of them. More important, you know that power lunches and power dinners have more in common than not.

"Three or four hours and a hundred or two hundred more dollars."

You spend more, you'll get more. And won't your partner be proud of you!

More power (dinners) to you!

"Somehow Stanton, I don't think this is the appropriate setting to go over the merger proposal."

Chapter Fourteen

Power Lunches Within Your Company

How to Power Lunch Your Boss

14

Let me tell you about an anxiety-producing experience I had at a "company power lunch" several years ago.

At the time, I was Eastern Sales Manager for the Chicago Division of one of the world's most highly visible corporations. My boss, the General Manager and Executive Vice-President, was headquartered in Chicago; I worked in Manhattan.

At least every two months, I'd spend a week or so in Chicago, calling on the Midwest managers of clients to gain their help in swaying their New York corporate headquarters to buy what my eastern reps had to sell. At least once or twice during that week, the Chicago Executive Vice-President and I would dine together, sometimes with his wife, and we'd have at least one business lunch in the corporation's executive dining room. "He" was a black-belt of power lunch, though that name would never have occurred to him.

The dining room was relatively small, with a cocktail area of upholstered chairs, a bench and small tables. The chef was a master, and the drinks that were served weren't designed to skimp on the liquor bill.

This particular lunch took place in the executive dining room on my last day in town for that trip, and the boss also invited the local sales manager to join us. We had a couple of cocktails while discussing local and national sales situations, and then the boss stood, which was our signal to proceed to the adjacent dining area for lunch. We sat at three adjoining chairs at one side of a round table that could accommodate eight in great comfort. The meal included green salad, rolls and butter, small rare sirloins, fresh asparagus, roasted potatoes, dessert cheese and coffee. We talked all through the meal about the same sales situations.

The boss finally stood and told the local sales manager he wanted to have a word with me alone. After the "local" departed, the boss and I returned to the cocktail area where he offered, and I declined, an after-dinner drink.

"Mel," he said, "some other divisions are asking corporate headquarters for eastern sales managers like you. Headquarters turned them down because of the high cost. And it's turned out that since they can't have a man like you in their divisions, I can't have one any longer, either.

"You're fired!"

He, my boss, was the "luncher," and I turned out to be the unsuspecting "lunchee." What a power lunch!

E. Melvin Pinsel
Co-Author

Things turned out very well, however. After my boss' personal apologies for the situation and an offer for me to return to Chicago and resume my previous responsibilities, I asked to use the phone at the side of the bench. I reached the New York V.P. who headed the sales-rep division of the corporation, and they put a new title on my office door. I was back in business in two minutes — despite being initially taken aback by the first announcement.

'TIS A WISE SON WHO KNOWS HIS OWN FATHER

Important business lunches transpire every day between executives of the same company. Careers hinge on many of them. Wise executives figure out quickly whether they are the luncher or the lunchee.

Everything you've read so far about power lunching applies to company lunches. An outside lunch may focus on one deal, large or small, and the inside lunch may concern your career as a whole and your growth within the company — matters near and dear to everyone. But you can look at them as being quite similar.

For instance, you should regard your company as another good client, someone with whom you are already doing a great deal of business. Perhaps you're earning $25,000, $55,000, $155,000 or $250,000 a year from your company. You are a supplier, and if you've been with the company for a while, your business (salary or commission or both) has increased. Your company is not only your employer, *it's your most critical account!*

So let's operate under the correct assumption that a company lunch, like a business lunch, can be turned into a successful power lunch. We'll generally follow this book's chapters down the line and discuss how they apply to what we will now refer to as the "company power lunch." For the present, though, let's assume your company doesn't have an internal executive dining room.

THE COMPANY POWER LUNCH

You've seen it a thousand times. Around 11:30 a.m., Bill in marketing calls Tom in product management and says something like, "Hey, you want to grab a sandwich and a beer at noon?" Sound familiar? Sure, you read it back in Chapter One.

Bill's motivation for calling Tom is the same as the seller calling the buyer. Bill the Seller wants to make a "profitable" deal with Tom the Buyer. Of course, there will be no exchange of money or goods, but the motivation remains the same — gain.

Gain, here, is used in the sense that the seller wants to know something that's going on in the buyer's department that will help him within the company. Or he wants to learn how the company is positioning itself in some area with which he isn't very familiar. Or any of a hundred other areas in which Bill the Seller feels Tom the Buyer can be of help (spell that G-A-I-N) to him.

Nothing wrong with that.

Bill and Tom may be close or casual business friends or simply two guys who labor in the same vineyard. But as long as Bill feels the desire to invite Tom to a company business lunch, everything that has been discussed in this book applies to turn the occasion into a company power lunch.

WHO TO INVITE

The purposes of the company power lunch are greatly varied, and often determine your choice of guests. Sometimes, it's easier to affect a power lunch with a party outside your company than within. Outside the company, you know the particular clients or prospects, while within your own firm there may be many levels, areas, responsibilities and authorities that give you concern.

Remember, your company is your *most critical account*. Treating the company in that light will help you understand who to invite and how to do so. When *you* initiate a company power lunch, the reason for the lunch primarily will determine who you invite, and why you may add to the list on a secondary or tertiary basis.

Whether your company is a multinational conglomerate or consists of a handful of people, inviting the boss to lunch won't go unnoticed. Yet there is hardly a boss around who doesn't appreciate aggressive attitudes toward increasing or improving his business. If you issue the invitation to the boss on the basis of, "I've got an idea on plant expansion in Taiwan or cost reduction in the shipping room," he won't turn down the *discussion*. To keep him from turning down the *lunch*, suggest the meal as a way to discuss the subject without losing time from the regular business day. Besides, the restaurant *you* choose is nearby, and you'll both be back by 1:30. Again, remember the concept of your company being the largest buyer of your services, and treat the boss in essentially the same manner you would treat another good client. Like the outside client, he'll know he's there for business reasons and will act accordingly. Also, make sure he knows the check is yours!

Of course, if the person you invite to a company power lunch is at your corporate level or below, you immediately hold good cards. In short, you can establish and maintain control without much difficulty. It's unlikely your claim on the driver's seat will be challenged.

Drive carefully, but drive on!

THE STRATEGY

You know the Robert Burns quote: "The best laid plans of mice and men gang aft a'gley." The quote has been around a long time, even though its concept is wrong. There's no question that outside circumstances beyond your control can affect a company power lunch. If the roof falls in — really falls in — there's not much you can do. Steak a-la-roofing-tile won't get you anywhere. But the quote is wrong because it refers to "best laid" plans. If you do your best to plan the strategy of a company power lunch, it generally won't go astray.

As in any power lunch, you must know as much as possible about the person who will be the target for your presentation. Perhaps he's your boss or the division head of a corporate branch. He may be officed in a city a thousand miles away. But in the same way you wouldn't take your best outside prospect to a power lunch without doing your homework on his likes and dislikes, his hobbies and his politics, you must know the same things about your target within your company. Doing research, which we emphasized in Chapter Three, remains a key task. Don't slight it. However, take note of some differences:

1. In an outside power lunch, you occasionally can get by with a little B.S. Perhaps you're bragging a bit, or you don't really know the answer to a question. Sure, you should be more honest, but you cover with some verbal sleight of hand.

Don't ever do that at a company power lunch. Whether your guest is above, alongside or beneath you in the company's echelon, it's too easy for him to check on any statement you make. If you don't do your homework well enough or if you don't know the answer to a question, stay honest and say so! Add that you'll have all the facts tomorrow or whenever, and then *get those facts*, even if you have to enlist the troops for an all-night session. Honesty should be your *only* policy, especially within your own company.

2. In Chapter Three, we discussed "staffing up." At an outside power lunch, that's sometimes desirable, and other times hard to avoid. If on the outside your invited guest wants to include his sales manager, you might want to bring yours, too.

At a company power lunch, it behooves you not to bring

others. If you want to invite the marketing director and he accepts, but suggests he bring the head of research along, that's usually that! On the outside, you might want to counter with a "partner" of your own, but things aren't that simple inside the company. You don't want it to appear you're building a clique or beginning a "palace revolt." Keep *your* ideas for the company power lunch your own, and you alone will have the power.

WOMEN AND THE COMPANY LUNCH

If you're a woman in business, you probably agree with what you read in Chapter Four. And at a company power lunch, the concept of "total control" is multiplied.

Of course, you still might be suspected of motives other than pure business, particularly if your guest is the boss or any other person on a higher corporate level than you. Big deal! You've faced that problem your entire business life, and it's probably going to be a long time before the woman in business is treated as a true equal. Re-read Chapter Four and apply everything you learned to the company power lunch. It's virtually the same game, but with some different plays. However, you will have an additional, very important concern. Sometimes a business woman has a better reputation for taking control of a situation in the minds of people *outside* her company than among those she shares the corporate banner with. A power lunch will go far toward building your reputation in that area. You now have an opportunity to display to your guest something they may not have sufficiently noticed: Your ability to take total charge of a situation. It can be a great opportunity!

One point in Chapter Four deals with losing that last power point by allowing the "man" to put you in a taxi or share a cab with you, and then paying the tab for the both of you. It's a power loss you must avoid, and the chapter discussed how to do that. The same strategy remains for the company power lunch if you are dining outside the corporate dining room. Though you have picked up the check and tips in the restaurant, being from the same office as your guest opens the door for him to more easily suggest you share a cab back — and then he'll grab the fare. Don't let it happen! Do the same

"Then it's settled. We kick ass and take names."

as in Chapter Four — walk off alone or take a cab for yourself on the pretense of an upcoming appointment at another office.

Another crucial note: If your guest is another woman, *don't* let your guard down and treat her as a "sister." You may have more in common with her than your male counterparts, but she's simply another boss, supervisor or co-worker who you must treat in the same manner as your male guests. You've got a lot to lose by letting your secrets slip out to her.

CHOOSING THE RESTAURANT

By now, it's apparent the company power lunch differs from the outside power lunch only by degree. But some of those subtle differences are significant. For instance, each of us probably has some behavior patterns that differ from established company patterns. Of course, your behavior must be sufficiently in line or you wouldn't be employed by your boss. Remember, though, that you're playing in *his* ballpark, and you've got to score runs according to the rules he sets.

In choosing a restaurant for an outside power lunch, your options are limited only by such factors as your client's preferences and your ability to exercise control in a particular restaurant. However, in a company power lunch, your guest is most often going to be the boss or someone in a position higher than yours. The reason: You're setting up this lunch for gain — *your* gain — and that's generally available only from those above you.

Therefore, while it's fine to choose a "haute cuisine" restaurant for an outside power lunch, that might be a bad move for a company power lunch. If your firm is a very conservative organization, you may want to consider a type of restaurant that better reflects a conservative approach.

Check out, by lunching with a non-business friend, a couple of restaurants that fit such a description. When you find one or two, set yourself up with the owner or maitre d' as a V.I.P., both personally and in your corporate position. *How you're treated in the establishment will impress your boss or any other superior you invite there for a company power lunch.*

By the way, if you're inviting your boss, make sure the restaurant is not one he frequents more than you. You stand a chance of losing power if he's given a hearty welcome by the maitre d' instead of you, and all the staff's attention is focused on him.

But if you want to live a bit dangerously, you might follow the example of a company power lunch that co-author Mel Pinsel set up with his boss some years ago in Miami. He knew the boss liked a nearby power lunch-type membership restaurant. Both had personal memberships. Mel set the date for the lunch ten days in advance, using an excuse that his lunch calendar was filled until then, which was true. Yet most of his power lunches during that ten-day period were held in that same restaurant. The gratuities were a little heavier, the compliments on food and service more frequent.

When Mel and the boss held their meeting there ten days later, it was a *real* company power lunch. The boss was, of course, greeted cordially and properly, but Mel was treated like the King of Siam. Yes, even the boss can be impressed by the attention *you* receive from owners, maitre's d and captains in the best restaurants, particularly places where he is known. (By the way, Mel did get the raise he was after.)

Now let's deal with the role of the internal executive dining room. Basically, three types exist:

1. The large room where every employee is welcome. Service may be cafeteria-style or served at the table. No seating distinction is made between top management or clerical personnel. Often the meal is company-subsidized to keep the cost low, or it's served free. No alcoholic beverages are offered.

2. The "divided" dining room. Staff and clerical personnel are served in one area, usually bare table-style. The same menu is offered in an adjacent area for executive-level personnel, but tablecloths are used and seating arrangements are more comfortable. No company subsidy is involved, but meal costs are set on a not-for-profit basis. No alcoholic beverages are served.

3. The private executive dining room. Serves executive-level personnel, by invitation and reservation only. The size ranges from accommodations for six to eight, up to any number within reason. It may also be used for client business

lunches. It's usually well-appointed. It may offer the choice of two or three entrees or have a fixed menu for the day. There's no charge to diners because the operation is a company write-off. Unless company policy prohibits, alcoholic beverages are available.

For the purposes of the company power lunch, each of these types of internal corporate dining rooms present a basic problem. Remember, the primary reason for the power lunch, inside or outside the company, is to have your guest's full attention, away from typical office distractions. Though you're technically at lunch in the first two types of dining rooms, there are too many opportunities for interruption by internal phone calls or people coming over to ask questions or make comments.

So if you want, for whatever reason, to dine with company employees in dining rooms of the first two types, be aware they don't offer optimum opportunities for a company power lunch. It may be beneficial to be seen eating with So-and-So, but there's little chance to exercise the power you want to use.

On the other hand, the private executive dining room is where you can demonstrate your ability to control a situation. Just the title of the room tells a lot: You've arrived at a certain corporate level. You've been given special privileges commensurate with your sizable contribution to the company. Sure, there may be a risk of interruptions by telephone calls, but no more than at any commercial restaurant. And in a private executive dining room, as in public establishments, you can advise management you aren't available for calls.

If your executive dining room is of the small type, where only a maximum of 10 or so people can be served, *you* are in total control because you set up the meeting. A true company power lunch.

Should the dining room accommodate two, three or more tables, you're faced with problems similar to those encountered in commercial restaurants. Your options, however, are simple. Because you have spent time getting to know and demonstrating your appreciation for the dining room staff, you'll be able to arrange for the best table in the room. The maitre d' will pay sufficient attention to your table's needs. However, don't push your luck if the chairman of the board is lunching with a group that same day.

The executive dining room can be a great place to try a ploy that almost always makes points with the "bosses" at your table, as well as with other diners in the room. *Without* looking at your watch, slide your chair back slightly from the table after coffee has been served, look at your guests and say softly, "I enjoyed our talk. Thanks! But I've got to finish that projection for P. G. See you later."

Then leave!

Even if P.G. is at your table, use the same plan!

The executive dining room is primarily used for exchanging ideas among top people within the company. It also affords you the chance to challenge the typically mundane attitudes of such places by demonstrating how to orchestrate an effective power lunch. Keep it "private," and keep it "profitable."

THE RESTAURANT STAFF

Remember what restaurateur and educator Gordon Sinclair said in Chapter Six: "If you want nothing to go wrong in a restaurant, and if your life depended on it, you would behave differently than if you were just going on a social lunch with somebody."

That observation carries extra weight with the company power lunch!

The power lunch, of course, is an exercise of *your* power. Chapter Six, dealing with the restaurant staff, describes how this power is accumulated and exercised. When your guest is from within your own company, whether placed higher or lower than you, he gets an opportunity to see your expertise in use. Though you control a power lunch as far as your *guest* is concerned, you must be certain to have full control of your assistants — the restaurant staff. The reflection *upon you* is most important.

However, in your desire to demonstrate your control to your boss or others from within your company, don't go overboard and become a showoff. Exercise your control with cool, and your well-prepared restaurant staff will make you look great.

SEATING ARRANGEMENTS

Chapter Seven, dedicated to this subject, says it all. Simply substitute your "company" guest for the "outside" guest and you have the answers. All, that is, except one. That is, how do you handle seating in a private executive dining room?

If the dining room is small and has only one table, and your guest is anyone but the boss, take for yourself the seat usually held by the boss. Obviously, it will be the most powerful seat at the table. And it won't hurt you with your company guest to have him see you sitting in the boss' chair. Reflected power is power you can use.

In this same type of corporate dining room when your boss is your guest, let him have his favorite seat. If he's right-handed, maneuver yourself to sit at his immediate left. If he's left-handed, sit at his right. In each case, his head will tend to turn toward you. If the dining room offers more than one table, use the same techniques as outlined in Chapter Seven.

There is, however, one additional power opportunity that usually isn't present in a public restaurant or club. Learn from the captain, maitre d' or manager what other corporate executives are dining in the room that day. Then you have the option of sitting close to a table of people you want to be near, or away from a table of people you'd rather stay your distance from.

BOOZE AT THE COMPANY LUNCH

Liquor is a fact of life, and it's certainly a factor in power lunching. It's even more of a factor in a company power lunch, whether it's present or absent.

When setting up a company power lunch at an outside restaurant or executive dining room, take a conservative approach. If your guest is the boss and you know he has taken a drink at lunch on other occasions, still play it safe. Don't say, "I'll order drinks now." It's better to say, "Mr. Goller, would you like a drink before lunch?" If the answer is yes, proceed. If he asks if you are going to have one, say, "Yes, I think we have time for just one as we look at the menu. Will you join me?"

You've displayed your power, but you haven't put the company imprint on the "three martini lunch." Nothing could be further from a company power lunch than a meal of the three-martini variety. Don't suggest a second or third drink unless it's at his request, and even then take a conservative attitude and politely decline if a third drink is suggested. Though you are in control, he may be running a little test. Skip the drink; pass the test.

Watch how your corporate guest's actions either conform to or vary from the stated company policy concerning drinks. If there is any conflict, opt to follow company policy.

"Coffee, please!"

THE MENU

In essence, everything described in Chapter Nine about the menu and meal applies to a power lunch within your own company. If the lunch is in your private executive dining room, the process is even simpler. Your menu choices are more limited and drinks before lunch aren't a concern if liquor isn't available. And certainly, the table manners described in Chapter Nine apply anywhere, anytime.

But should your power lunch take place outside the private dining room, you do have some opportunities to exercise power. Go for the power items on the menu. If your guest is the boss, don't let his ordering a white wine spritzer keep you from ordering Scotch on the rocks. Still, don't exceed one drink more than what he orders.

Should he order Salad Nicoise, select rare sirloin with crisp cottage fries. Your boss will look up to you for not kow-towing to him in following his menu choices, and he will admire the macho lunch you have chosen.

You might, however, consider leaving a fair amount of steak and potatoes uneaten. Place your knife and fork side by side in the center of your plate. The waiter will know you are finished with your meal. If the boss is still eating, he may look over and ask, "Everything okay?" Your answer: "Yes, of course. I enjoyed the steak. But I'm anxious to discuss the Atay deal with you."

Again, you are controlling what transpires at the table, and your boss can't help but know you must do the same with clients or prospects. Result: You've gained power. Remember, one of the main objectives of the company power lunch with someone in a higher corporate position is to display your use of strategy and control. Let him see how effectively you operate.

Here's a tip concerning the close of a company power lunch. As you wouldn't consider letting your client or prospect pick up the check, do the same here. None of this, "Let's share this one, Tom," or, "It all goes on the same expense account." Your power — Your check!

Be very careful if you are an executive with a company credit card. If you are not paying with cash (which would avoid any problems in this area), tell the waiter or captain so your guest may hear, "Please charge these meals to my *personal* American Express account."

Remember: Straight arrows score more often.

DOWN TO COMPANY BUSINESS

If ever this phrase applies, it applies at the company power lunch. Let's assume your guest is in a higher position of responsibility than you. It certainly is within the realm of common courtesy to talk lightly of social subjects such as sports, weather and the market. If he should be sufficiently aware of your personal situation — and you of his — houses, gardens, cars and boats are subjects that can fill a few preliminary moments.

But as much as an outside-the-company guest knows it's a business meeting, your boss also knows the subject is business. You may have had to disclose the topic you wish to discuss in order to set up the company power lunch. In that case, after all other items of importance to the successful power lunch are implemented, ease into the matter early. "Jack, I'm glad we could take time together to discuss the new EDP application to loan processing that the company is about to put on line. May I suggest we order a drink, look at menus and then we can get immediately to the idea I have, and your reactions to it.

How can he say no?

If, as in an outside power lunch, your guest wants to talk about the company from "his point of view," open your eyes wide, your ears wider and give him your full attention. You're getting the "power lunch bonus" — insights into things he knows that you don't. What's more he's becoming closer and demonstrating his trust in you. Wow — are you going to have power.

But don't get so caught up in his discussion, which may be self-serving, that you forget the business of the power lunch — *your* business! Order coffee, lean slowly forward and say in a soft voice, "Let's talk now about the ideas I have about EDP and loan processing."

Gotcha!

THE COMPANY DINNER

There are few reasons for having a company business dinner except when some corporate executives are out of town together at a convention or seminar. In those cases, a company *power* dinner is impractical. At both conventions and seminars, you're usually too tired at the end of the day to be at your best. And even today, conventions still lend themselves to too much liquor. Assuming you'd be able to find the proper type of restaurant and make all the arrangements necessary for a power lunch, the odds are it would be overbooked for the convention.

As for other company dinners, trying to turn them into power dinners is too risky because you might come off as pushing too hard within the company. Hold the power dinners for clients and prospects as described in Chapter Fourteen. Keep the company dinner for that special occasion when you want to sincerely compliment the boss or a superior, or when it's a gracious and unpresumptuous way of saying, "Thank you." And make sure the dinner's cost is personally paid by you, not charged to your company expense account.

Chapter Fifteen

Common Errors, Mistakes and Screw-ups

Power Disasters: The Long and Short of it

15

You've calculated all the strategy and made proper plans for the power lunch to end all power lunches. You're prepared for any eventuality. Not even a minor foul-up is possible, you say, much less a major screw-up.

Following are the most obvious mistakes. Obvious because they seem almost too basic to worry about . . . and this is a major difference between business lunchers and power lunchers: veteran power lunchers concern themselves with *every* detail.

When your client orders a Napoleon for dessert, say you'll skip dessert and then tell him your doctor's latest warning about obesity.

Combine any two of the following moves and you're guaranteed to turn your gem of a power lunch into the wimp lunch to end all wimp lunches:

Invite your client's boss, but don't tell your regular contact about it.

Bring your guest to a restaurant where the maitre d' knows you very well as the diner who likes to sit in the back corner with his young niece.

Tell your prospective guest that you've heard he prefers doing business at three-martini lunches. Then take him to one of those joints that serves crummy food and unlimited drinks at a package price.

Don't give a thought to how the lunch will go. You've met your guest before, and you know everything will go well by itself.

179

Don't bother researching your guest's likes and dislikes. Don't worry about the type of restaurant or food he likes. If it's good enough for you, it's good enough for him.

Never check with your guest's secretary of 15 years. What would she know that could help you?

As a woman executive, play coy and demure. Don't let your male guest know you can exercise power. Or your female guest, either.

Take your prospect to the newest place in town. You know your personal charm will win you a good table without reservations, even though you've never been there before.

Demonstrate your power immediately to the captain after you're seated. Complain about a spot on your glass and a knife that has been improperly placed at your plate.

Snap your fingers at the first serving person within sight and call, "Hey, boy!"

When you leave with your guest at your side, tell the maitre d' you'll never return. Don't explain why, just storm out.

Don't worry that your table has your guest facing the kitchen entrance. Your conversation will compensate for the view.

If you are a female executive, show your feminity. Show *both* of them. Wear a very low-cut dress to lunch.

Set up your power lunch at a restaurant that has fine spaghettini made with olive oil and garlic. Wind the pasta on your fork fully, and slurp up what won't wind.

Let your guest choose where he will sit. It's just a business lunch.

Choose your seat based on which one has the best view of the river.

Order your first martini as a double. Order your second martini as a double. Order your third martini as a double.

When your guest says he'll have a white wine spritzer, tell him he should try a "man's drink" like yours.

Be sure to touch up your makeup at the table after you've asked for the check. After all, you want to look your best.

Top off the lunch with a diatribe about how many of the companies you deal with just don't understand "women's lib."

Knowing that your guest is well-placed in his company, suggest you make an afternoon of it and order a pitcher of Margaritas.

Why should you concern yourself with "power foods?" Order the diet salad and a Coke.

Ask your guest if he has change for a five dollar bill and some quarters.

Bring your best girl to dinner with your client and his wife, particularly when he knows you're married.

Set up an after-dinner theater date for your client and his wife. Who cares if you have to rush through the meal and run for the curtain? They'll enjoy the show.

Ask your guest if he would like to get laid after dinner.

Tell your female prospect that your wife wouldn't understand your business lunch with her. Touch her hand softly.

Brag to your guest, male or female, of your sexual conquests.

Question your client's decision to order his steak "medium." You know "rare" is the only way to go.

When your client orders a Napolean for dessert, say you'll skip dessert and then tell him your doctor's latest warning about obesity.

Go quickly and heavily into your pitch as soon as you and your client are seated.

Make sure your guest is aware this is a very expensive restaurant, and you didn't invite him here to enjoy the food.

During coffee, make your presentation strong and long. Especially long. After all, it's Friday, isn't it?

When the time seems ripe to talk business, reach for your attache case and pull out the whole computer run. All 84 pages of it.

When the check is improperly presented so that your guest has a chance to go for it, let him take it. He's got more money than you.

Don't let your client think you're cheap; show him the total of the check.

When lunching in Tampa, make sure your prospect understands the restaurant would never make it in New York.

When lunching in New York, make sure your prospect understands that the check would cover four business lunches in Tampa.

Regardless of local custom, set the lunch meeting for one o'clock in the afternoon.

Forget receipts. If the comptroller doesn't like it, you can go to the company president.

The IRS isn't going to go into such small matters as your notations regarding who you took to lunch or for what business purpose. Who does the IRS think it is?

Take the boss to lunch at the local "scream and holler" deli. Show him how cost-conscious you are.

Take the boss to the most expensive place in town. Ask to borrow twenty bucks for the maitre d'.

In the company's executive dining room, ask the boss why he's always in such a rush to return to his office.

You're good, but only a one-man operation. How could you think of a business lunch at "21"?

Don't expect the maitre d' at a top power lunch spot to pay any attention to you. Your tips and understanding don't rank with the guys from the Fortune 500 companies.

Never fail to ask for a doggie bag!

QUICK THINKING

Don't worry, you may be saying to yourself. You'd never make such foolish errors. But nothing in life is perfect. Even the best-prepared plans of veteran power lunchers sometimes go awry, and occasionally meals degenerate into downright disasters. What really tests the mettle of a power luncher, though, is how they handle the disasters and turn them into advantages. Here are some examples of potential horror stories that ended up with happy endings because of quick thinking.

Generally, it's a poor tactic to use the title "doctor" when making reservations where you aren't well-known because American doctors have a notoriously bad reputation among restaurant staffs for being poor tippers. So instead of carrying clout, the doctor title usually will get you the *worst* table, not the best.

But there are instances when the doctor title has worked. Listen to one expert Midwest power luncher: "I have a surgeon friend — let's call him Dr. Smith — and one evening he happened to be having dinner with another person at the table next to mine. The waiter arrived, and I asked for a particular entree. The waiter said, "I'm sorry, but the last one was taken by Dr. Smith,' indicating my friend at the next table. I looked at the waiter and said, 'How long have I been coming here?' 'A long time, sir,' he replied. 'Well, I've never told you that I am also a doctor.' The waiter was amazed, and I'll be damned if he just didn't bring out the whole dish and split it among us.

"On another occasion, I was taken to a famous steak place in Chicago by some out-of-towners. Since the restaurant was very crowded, I said, 'You can pick up the check, but *I'll* get the table.' What are you going to do? These were all New Yorkers — big hitters who think they know how to operate in restaurants. So I said, 'Just hang back.' I forced our way through the crowd and said, 'Do you have that table for Dr.

Walker?' The guy said, 'Sure, I'm glad you got here! We almost had to give it away.' He didn't know me from Adam, but this was one case where the doctor title helped."

Another long-time power luncher recalled his technique of obtaining reservations at restaurants when he was young and had no connections. "I simply called up and said in a forceful manner, 'Hello, this is Dr. Hart. I'll be coming in with a party of six, and I know you will take good care of us, *as usual.*"

In short, use the doctor title only if you can carry it off with aplomb!

Another incident illustrating how potential disaster can be turned into an advantage was related by Gerard Brach, a Houston restaurant entrepreneur and consultant, who reminisced about the days he worked for Restaurant Associates in New York. It's a story about one of the most unusual exits ever made from an uncomfortable lunch situation:

"This happened at the Hemisphere Club at the top of the Time-Life Building in New York. One of our members was Charlie Bluhdorn of Gulf & Western, rest his soul. Charlie was gobbling up everybody in mergers at the time. He was a very aggressive man, as you can well imagine, and people were kind of terrorized.

"He had a luncheon party on the 47th floor in Room G. The occasion was a particular outfit being gobbled or regobbled, and there was a man in the party who was very reluctant about venturing into the room with the Bluhdorn people and their sharp, protruding teeth and sharkskin suits. Members of the party arrived — you could tell they were the gobblees, not the gobblers — and this particular man looked ashen grey. Evidently, he didn't want to go in because he said, 'I don't know if I want to go through with it, this thing really goes against the grain,' etc., etc. Although he almost seemed to have a physical repugnance to going through with it, his friends convinced him.

"So the lunch started. They had a very quick bar, and were seated at an E-shaped table, with the gobblers and gobblees sitting at the head of the table and the underlings at the three legs of the E. I felt sorry for this guy because Mr. Bluhdorn was not the most enticing of characters: He had

teeth like Lauren Hutton (but on him they didn't look good) and big lips. This, along with his heavy German accent, almost made him like a cartoon — but he was very real.

"Anyway, this man was sweating throughout the whole affair. Bluhdorn was talking to him, one of Bluhdorn's lieutenants was talking to him, he was sweating and his friends were prodding him all through the lunch. Suddenly, I saw this incredible look of relief on his face. He raised his salad fork to his mouth, bit and then suddenly howled and threw his chair back. I shot over to pick him up while he's on the floor saying, "It bit me! It bit me!' Attached to his lower lip was half of a cricket.

"Somehow the cricket got chopped in half, probably by the salad man, and it was very upset. So the cricket, blinded by French dressing and not feeling well, attacked this quivering, pale lip and it drew blood. Now, I don't believe a one-tenth ounce cricket could knock a 180-pound man off his chair, but he hurled himself backward and was lying on the floor screaming practically in delight. He got the cricket off his lip — it *was* bloody — and he was showing the cricket to everybody, including Bluhdorn, as if it were a wholly owned subsidiary of Gulf & Western. Then he showed the bloody napkin and stormed out of there.

"It was the most interesting thing I've even seen: It *was* truly hurting him, but it was also his way out. And he *was* relieved. I've never known a man look so relieved!"

What if there's a *real* disaster? In a restaurant, that usually means spilled food or drink.

A female public relations executive from Minneapolis relates: "Once in California, a waitress spilled an entire tray of margaritas all over the only dress I had with me. So I had to put on a waiter's uniform and go to every cleaner in Santa Monica trying to get my dress cleaned and pressed immediately. We never ate. But my client went with me, laughing all the way."

There was another woman, though, who didn't handle her power lunch well. In fact, she let feminism get the best of her, and killed the lunch before it started. This story is by a New York real estate executive:

"I believe feminism didn't kill common courtesy. There will always be a civilized way of living. Once, a lady invited me to lunch with a young lawyer. I made arrangements to pick her up in my car. I arrived, saw her waiting for me, stopped and got out of the car. I opened the passenger door for her and returned to the driver's seat. She proceeded to read me the riot act: 'I don't *ever* want you to do that again!' I was shocked, apologized for offending the principles she lived by and simply said, 'Why don't you tell me where you would like to be dropped off, since I don't think we will get along.'

"She obviously took my behavior as being condescending, while I was merely trying to be civil. I'm sorry, but I'm from the last generation that believes in civilized behavior. 'You still react to everything based on one set of principles, and that's a sign of immaturity,' I told her. I said she had the potential of being a great lady when she got older, but as a young person she was simply too inflexible to be a well-rounded person."

Sometimes even the most powerful lunch can be ruined by an accountant, a former employee of the IRS relates:

"There was the case where a major public relations firm took a prospective client to lunch at a top New York restaurant. When the client arrived with a small entourage, the agency principal was there as well as his chief account people, sitting in a private room. The waiter came in and took a drink order, luncheon was served and business was conducted. Everything was absolutely wonderful and tremendously impressive, and that lasted until the monthly bill from the agency came to the client, and on the bill was a charge for the luncheon. The *client* was charged for this great show at the club. That was one of the most stupid moves in the world!

"If you're ever going to do that, there has got to be a way to bury that charge over the months — or you should consider it a cost of doing business."

The moral: Never, never let the client pay.

Finally, Stanley Stewart, a Midwest corporate executive and inveterate power luncher, has an amusing example of how assertively outrageous behavior can sometimes be used to get what you want out of a recalcitrant staff — and avert disaster.

"Following fashion, reservations, had been made at the Blue Fox in San Francisco for 'dinner for four' at 9 p.m. We arrived at 8:45 p.m. and were asked to have a nonexistent seat in a tiny holding bar. I was dressed in a white suit, white shoes and shirt with a multi-colored ascot.

"We sat in the holding bar area until 10:15 p.m., when we were called for our 9 p.m. reservation. As we walked toward the dining room, a maitre d' stopped me. 'Sir,' he said, 'You must have a tie on to enter the dining room.' Having waited for an hour and fifteen minutes in the bar, I just stared at him for a moment. My measured reply was, 'Since when doesn't an ascot qualify as a tie, and why would you tell me now when I have been in the restaurant for more than an hour?' By this time, the already-seated guests were becoming interested in the standoff and I was about to lose.

"I looked as mean as I could and said, 'I'll be right back.' Retiring to the men's lounge, I undid my ascot and tied it into a gigantic bow tie (thank God for a creative spark at the right moment!) Taking the arms of my guests gently, I moved back into the 'combat area.'

"We are ready to be seated,' I said with so much authority that the 'penguin' probably felt as if I were an IRS agent asking about unreported cash tips. He stared and stared some more. Finally, he lowered his eyes. 'This way, sir . . . ,' he said.

"Every patron in the restaurant stood and applauded my bow tie. What a joy to beat down an arrogant maitre d' just once!"

Chapter Sixteen

The Great American Power Lunch Test

Update and Scorecard

16

Remember the old song the health-nuts always sang . . .

"You are what you eat"

Not wrong for health-nuts, but even more right for power lunchers!

Setting up a power lunch and running it well must be accompanied by food and drink choices that continue the display of your power.

What follows is a simple list of many items commonly found on restaurant menus. Treat this as a test of your understanding of "Power food and drink". After a review of Chapter 8, *Liquor and the Power Lunch* and Chapter 9, *The Menu and the Meal*, you should be aware of which food and beverage will enhance your image as a power luncher. Fill in a "P" to indicate power food or drink and a "W" to indicate a wimp. When you have finished, turn to the back of the book and see how well you did when compared to the experts. Only a score of 100% is acceptable if you really want to make a power lunch work for you.

Remember, you are what you eat in front of your client, prospect or co-workers at a power lunch.

Anchovies	___	Artichoke leaves	___
Apple pie	___	Fresh asparagus	___
Apple pie with sharp cheddar	___	Aspics	___
		Avocado	___
Applesauce	___	Bacon	___
Artichokes	___	Banana Bread	___

Beef Bourgenion	——	Camembert	——
Beef Oskar	——	Edam	——
Beef Stew	——	Feta or other Greek	——
Beef Stroganoff	——	Goat Cheese	——
Beef Wellington	——	Gouda	——
Black bean soup	——	Gruyere	——
Bloody Mary	——	Limburger	——
Blueberries	——	Mozzarella	——
Blueberry muffins	——	Muenster	——
Blueberry pie	——	Roquefort	——
Bourbon, rocks or neat	——	Stilton	——
Broccoli	——	Chicken ala king	——
Brook trout	——	Chicken Kiev	——
Brussel sprouts	——	Chicken livers	——
Butt steak	——	Chicken paprikash	——
Cabbage	——	Chicken pot pie	——
Calamari	——	Fried chicken	——
Calves liver	——	Chiffon pie	——
Cantalope	——	Chili	——
Capers	——	Hot Chocolate	——
Casseroles	——	Chocolate Cake	——
Cassoulet	——	Chocolate Mousse	——
Catfish	——	Cioppino	——
Beluga Caviar	——	Clam or fish chowder	——
Caviar and vodka	——	Steamed clams	——
Celery root	——	Stuffed clams	——
Chateaubriand	——	Club soda	——
Cheeses:		Coffee cake	——
American	——	Coke	——
Bel Paese	——	Cole slaw	——
Bleu	——	Any combination platter	——
Brie	——		

192

Conch	——	Goose liver pate	——
Coquille St. Jacques	——	Grilled breast of goose	——
Cous-cous	——		
Corned beef	——	Grapefruit	——
Corned beef hash	——	Guacamole	——
Cornish hen	——	Baked ham	——
Crab legs	——	Country smoked ham	——
Crab Louis	——		
Soft shell crabs	——	Hamburger steak	——
Crepes	——	Hasenpfeffer	——
Crepes Suzette	——	Hearts of palm	——
Daquiri	——	Herring	——
Date nut bread	——	Horseradish dressing	——
Duck (half)	——		
Duck — rare sliced breast	——	Hushpuppies	——
		Ice Cream	——
Eggs Benedict	——	Iced sherbet	——
Stuffed eggs	——	Irish Whiskey, rocks or neat	——
Eggplant	——		
English mixed grill	——	Kidney beans	——
Espresso	——	Kiwi fruit	——
Filet	——	Lamb curry	——
Fish & chips	——	Rack of lamb	——
Flambe "anything"	——	Rack of lamb en croute	——
Flan	——	Rare lamb chops	——
Fondues (any)	——		
French fries	——	Lasagna	——
French onion soup	——	Lettuce Wedge	——
Fresh fruit and brie	——	Lillet	——
Frog legs	——	Lima beans	——
Fruit compote	——	Long Island iced tea	——
Fruit based mixed drinks	——	Lobster (half or whole)	——
		Lobster bisque	——
Gin, rocks or neat	——	Lobster Newberg	——

193

Lobster tails	____	Pickles	____
London broil	____	Pineapple	____
Manhattan	____	Polenta	____
Margarita	____	Pork chops	____
Marinated sliced fruit	____	Pork shank	____
Martini	____	Pork tenderloin	____
Mahi mahi	____	Stuffed pork chops	____
Meat loaf	____	Potatoes:	
Melon balls	____	Baked	____
Minnestrone	____	Boiled	____
Muffins	____	Cottage fried	____
Wild mushrooms	____	French fried	____
Mussels	____	Mashed	____
Noodles & cheese	____	Souffle	____
Omelette	____	Pot roast	____
Onion rings	____	Prime rib	____
Osso Bucco	____	Prime rib, bone in	____
Baked oysters	____	Prosciutto and goat cheese	____
Fresh oysters and clams	____	Quiche	____
Fried oysters and clams	____	Ratatouille	____
Oyster mousse	____	Rhubarb	____
Paella	____	Rice pudding	____
Pancakes	____	Wild rice	____
Parfait	____	Salad bar	____
Pasta with sauce	____	Salads:	
Pears	____	Caesar salad	____
Pecan Pie	____	Carrot salad	____
Roasted peppers and anchovies	____	Chef salad	____
		Fruit salad	____
Perch	____	Greek salad	____
Perrier	____	Green salad with chunk roquefort	____
Pheasant	____	Hollywood salad	____
		Hot spinach	____

Salad Nicoise ——

Sliced tomato and
onion salad ——

Waldorf salad ——

Salami ——

Finger sandwiches ——

Sanka ——

Sauerkraut ——

Any sausage ——

Scotch, rocks or neat ——

Seafood:

Salmon en croute ——

Salmon steak ——

Smoked salmon
(no bagel) ——

Scottish smoked
salmon ——

Salt broiled
sea bass ——

Sashimi ——

Scallops ——

Japanese raw
scallops ——

Broiled scrod ——

Seafood crepes ——

Seafood gumbo ——

Shellfish cocktail ——

Shrimp cocktail ——

Shrimp gumbo ——

Shrimp de jonghe ——

Dover sole ——

Filet of sole ——

French fried squid ——

Stuffed sea bass ——

Sushi ——

Swordfish ——

Filet of turbot ——

Whitefish ——

7-Up ——

Shish-ke-bob ——

Smorgasboard ——

Souffles ——

Soups:

Baked onion soup ——

Lentil soup ——

Pea soup ——

Thin soups ——

Sour cream ——

Sourdough bread ——

Spaghetti ——

Spare ribs ——

Spinach ——

Squab ——

Squash ——

Steaks:

Sirloin — rare ——

Roquefort sirloin ——

Sirloin with whole
peppercorns ——

Steak Diane ——

Steak and eggs ——

Steak and kidney pie ——

Steak tartare ——

T-bone — rare ——

Filet ——

Stewed tomatoes
and okra ——

Strawberries ——

Strawberry
shortcake ——

Stuffed tomato or avocado	——	Veal kidneys	——
Succotash	——	Veal scallopini	——
Sweetbreads	——	Mixed vegetables	——
Swiss steak	——	Vegetable terrine in aspic	——
Tab	——	Vegetarian plate	——
Tea	——	Venison	——
Iced Tea	——	Vichyssoise	——
Broiled tomatoes	——	Vodka, rocks or neat	——
Roast tongue	——	Waffles	——
Tournedos	——	Watercress	——
Tuna Salad	——	Welsh rarebit	——
Turkey	——	Whiskey sour	——
Braised veal shank	——	White bread	——
Broiled veal chop	——	Zabaglione	——
Medallion of veal	——	Zucchini	——

Where Power Lunchers Meet

A Sampler Coast to Coast

17

POWER LUNCH RESTAURANTS

To point you in the right direction, we've compiled a list of restaurants that lend themselves to power lunching.

But keep in mind these restaurants were chosen as *representative* of the kind of establishment that fulfills the most criteria for a successful power lunch. These include:

1. Management concern for the desires of the power luncher.

2. Proper staff to execute management's concern for you and your business contacts.

3. Appropriate seating opportunities.

4. Overall atmosphere.

5. Kitchen and menu excellence.

6. Location.

A restaurant you might quite properly enjoy for social occasions might not meet the needs of a power lunch. Some places that make for pleasant dining don't measure up when you want to exercise power. However, many restaurants that rate high on the scale for power lunches also may serve well for purely social or gastronomic purposes.

We haven't covered every city. We know that if you're cutting a deal in Des Moines, Boston or Santa Barbara, the restaurant you select there is more important to you than the top spot in Manhattan. Using the procedures outlined in the book, you shouldn't have difficulty choosing an appropriate dining place.

Here then is a sampling coast to coast, with input from businessmen, restaurant experts and impartial surveys.

CHICAGO

Nick's Fishmarket
Monroe at Dearborn
312/621-0200

Privacy is assured at this top Power Lunch location by the large leather booths, and the understanding by the staff of the necessities of a business lunch. Each booth has its own dimmer switch for business or romance.

Fish, seafood, and drinks are the order of the day; and all are very well presented, as well as perfectly prepared.

Expect to see and be seen by some of the city's big guns, and the better heeled and informed from out of town.

Reservations as early as possible.

Very expensive.

Chez Paul
660 N. Rush
312/944-6680

Subdued elegance in a hundred year old mansion, once the home of Colonel McCormick of the Chicago Tribune.

Placement of each table in the two main downstairs dining rooms permits an exchange of conversation without problems. The rooms are light and airy, the silver and linen sparkle.

Fine French cuisine, good drinks, excellent service that can be tailored to your needs.

Business-at-table only second to the menu.

Reservations mandatory.

Expensive.

Hy's of Canada
100 E. Walton St.
312/649-9555

An expansive menu; much wood and leather make up the main dining room of this popular businessman's meeting place at mid-day. Privacy is no problem.

In addition to the main dining area, about twenty tables with deep leather chairs are available in the lounge area.

Menu selection in the lounge is limited to sliced-to-order prime beef, a significant Power Lunch entree; Eliminates your guest's need to pour over the menu.

The very experienced, professional, and attractive serving persons pay attention to your needs, and will follow instructions.

Reserve in the lounge as many days ahead as possible.

Expensive.

Le Perroquet
70 E. Walton St.
312/944-7990

You will first be cleared by the plain clothes guard on the ground floor before you proceed in the private elevator to the third floor restaurant.

No gimmicks here. An excellent kitchen provides some of this country's finest Continental cuisine in an atmosphere of unhurried luxury.

Voices are low; service is quiet and of the very best. All your instructions will be carried out to the letter.

Your guests will be impressed, and receptive to your suggestions.

Reservations days or weeks in advance; or have a great line for a last minute try.

Very expensive.

The Palm
181 E. Lake Shore Drive
312/944-0135

For the Power Luncher who wants to bring his guest to a loud, brash, bigger than life "New York Steak House."

The booths are wooden, the floor the same. The waiters act as if they all own real estate; but can be brought around firmly to do your bidding at your leisure. They are professional.

Everyone here is talking deals or divorce, and looking to see who's about.

If bigger is better; the steaks, lobster, cottage fries and drinks here are the best. An additional American menu is available.

Happy place to be, but don't expect anonymity.

Reservations a must.

Very expensive.

Crickets
100 E. Chestnut St.
312/280-2100

Just off famed Michigan Avenue, this clubby restaurant exists at lunch for the heavy hitters of many businesses and professions. Like New York's famed "21", the toys that hang from the ceiling represent the various businesses of the regular patrons, and their sports interests.

Stucco walls, leather chairs, lots of wood and brass combine for a warm and friendly atmosphere.

A most professional staff serves without flaw. Somewhat noisy and crowded. Be selective about your seating.

French and American cuisine.

Reservations a must.

Very Expensive.

HOUSTON

Tony's
1801 South Post Oak
713/622-6778

Family owned restaurant. Well-established, they know their clients. Very professional and they recognize the needs of power lunchers. Very well lit, there are no bad seats, everyone can see everyone. Beef is main food served.

Brenners
10911 Katy Freeway
713/465-2901

Steak house. Run by Mrs. Brenner. Business lunches and dinners. Mrs. Brenner has been cooking in the kitchen ever since she opened it. Very neat, all waitresses.

Very expensive.

La Lorraine
11920 J Westheimer
713/493-4454

Run by two Frenchmen. Small, local restaurant in west Galleria. French cuisine de terroire — provincial cuisine. All waiters.

Kyoto
14004 Memorial Drive
713/870-0096

Japanese. Very few Americans. Food is wonderful, authentic, atmosphere is wonderful. Very traditional service by waitresses in traditional kimonos and obis. No sushi bar, everything brought to the table. Japanese businessmen in town from Japan eat here. Excellent sashimi. Restaurant broken up into little booths, with rice paper everywhere.

PHILADELPHIA

La Panatiere
1602 Locust St.
215/546-5452

Fresh flowers on every table.

An old mansion converted to an elegant restaurant. Quiet, professional service. Ask and it shall be done.

The reserve of the building carries through to the stately dining and business opportunities. Plenty of room to talk.

A la Carte French menu

Very expensive.

Reservations mandatory.

The Garden
1617 Spruce St.
215/546-4555

Once the Philadelphia Music Academy, this four story brownstone serves an excellent menu, that ranges from France to California.

Very popular, somewhat crowded. Outdoor patio dining in summer. Good service. Many "Business' regulars.

Reservations suggested.

Expensive.

Downey's
526 S. Front St.
215/629-0525

It's on the waterfront with a bar in front.

The owner is ex-CBS corporate, and knows what you want. Be sure to ask first. The food is Irish and American . . . and good. Crowded, not quiet, but good for business purposes.

Private rooms upstairs.

Moderate.

ST. LOUIS

Anthony's
10 S. Broadway
314/231-2334

Very contemporary decor. Elegant. Very fine kitchen, to the French side. A lot of business lunches, and Power Lunches too. Serving teams will understand your business wishes when informed beforehand. Many media persons, and others with time to use for business or romance while the food is prepared to order.

Reservations.

Very expensive.

NEW YORK CITY

"21" Club
21 W. 52nd St.
212/582-7200

Accepted by all as a legend in the business of business. Although also a celebrity hangout, it is a businessman's dream of a Power Lunch center.

Downstairs is a bit noisy, with a huge bar, and checkered tablecloths covering the dining tables. Upstairs is an elegant dining room, with white linen cloths, and haute cuisine service.

Whichever level you choose, make your reservation as many days in advance as possible. The frequent customer gets the best action here. From the Maitre d', to the bartender, the captains and the waiters; all will work with you to help carry off a successful Power Lunch!

Menu ranges from game birds to classic French, with steaks and fish of the finest caliber. Also famous for the "21" burger.

Expensive.

Christ Cella Restaurant
160 E. 46th St.
212/697-2479

Nothing fancy here, except perhaps the prices. Wooden tables and wooden chairs. Some of the best steaks and lobsters in town. Man-sized drinks.

The waiters are professional, and will respect your wishes as to timing and service.

Plain walls and plain floors. Downstairs is the place to be; upstairs for upstarts. Many small open rooms make up the dining area. Downstairs is primarily a male bastion. Business is the principle language spoken.

Many regular patrons. Call in advance for first floor reservations.

Very expensive.

The Four Seasons
Seagram Building
99 E. 52nd St.
212/754-9494

A huge restaurant, with high ceilings and dramatic decor. Floor to ceiling chain draperies.

Two primary rooms. The Bar Room is more casual, in the old-fashioned grill-room style. The extra large Pool Room still permits a warm feeling, helped by the gently bubbling 20 foot square pool in the center of the room.

All the serving persons will work with you, given to understand your needs. The menu ranges from steaks to classic international.

Very comfortable seating. As the name suggests, the menu and decor changes with the seasons.

Very expensive.

La Cote Basque
5 E. 55th St.
212/688-6525

It has been said that the staff sizes up your net worth as you enter, and decides then and there on how much service you will expect and receive.

Making yourself known at this truly "International Set" restaurant will pay off for your Power Lunch. Very upscale French in decor, menu and pricing, it exudes quiet charm and old money.

Very comfortable seating. Quiet, impeccable service. Excellent kitchen.

If you are out to impress your guest, this is the place. Make sure beforehand that you are known to the Maitre d' and the Captains.

Very expensive.

Lutece
249 E. 50th St.
212/752-2225

A French restaurant with the warmth of an old French inn. Choose the small downstairs dining room.

No pretense here. A small menu features some of the best of Classic Continental cuisine, with the owner's individual touches.

Seating is good. Serving persons will accede to your every request. They all reflect a pride in their work and in the food and drink they serve.

Not the most popular business gathering spot. Because of this, you can turn this gourmet's delight to your own Power desires.

Very expensive.

LOS ANGELES

The Windsor
3198 West Seventh St.
213/382-1261

Enter here, and you'll feel you are in a private club. Oak walls, stained glass windows, quiet oil paintings.

The upholstered seats are luxurious. The whole place is quietly understated.

More than forty years old, the restaurant staff has seen them all.

Business is a language that is well-known here. The service staff will understand what you want when they are told beforehand. Waiters and Captains work in tandem.

Menu is Continental primarily, but not stuffy.

Expensive.

Jimmy's
201 Moreno Drive
Beverly Hills
213/879-2394

A beautiful people's restaurant. Most elegant, in the Beverly Hills manner. Celebrities everywhere.

Happy atmosphere.

Business deals going on at every other table.

Basic menu is Continental-French.

Service is done with a flourish. Understanding is given by staff to your Power needs in a professional way.

A well-established restaurant that lends itself to Power Lunch.

Expensive.

Ma Maison
8368 Melrose Ave.
Hollywood
213/655-1991

A small French Bistro is what comes to mind in this chic California/French restaurant.

The majority of tables are under a huge awning, surrounded by flowering plants.

A place to see and be seen, it's difficult not to notice a number of Hollywood Stars daily.

Service is excellent. Staff will understand your needs.

Menu is primarily nouvelle French.

Early reservations are a must.

Expensive.

The Tower
Transamerica Center
1150 S. Olive St.
213/746-1554

Oriental rugs and deep club chairs in the lounge set the tone for this restaurant that seems like a private club.

The atmosphere is hushed, the service close to impeccable. The view from the thirty-second floor is spectacular, when the smog is out.

Businessmen abound at many tables. Staff understands your desires, and will fulfill upon proper instruction.

Very comfortable seating.

Reservations necessary.

French cuisine.

Expensive.

L'Escoffier
The Beverly Hilton
9876 Wilshire Boulevard
213/274-7777

It is difficult to recommend this most excellent restaurant for Power Lunching, because they serve only Dinner.

When the occasion presents itself, the understated gray, rose, and burgundy color scheme, together with the velvet chairs and candelabra, make for a most impressive Power Dinner opportunity.

A penthouse setting is complemented by unhurried, professional service that add to make an evening to remember. Quiet music throughout the dining area. Very formal atmosphere.

Classic French cuisine.

Business discussion over coffee.

Very expensive.

DETROIT

Caucus Club
City National Bank Building
150 W. Congress Street
313/965-4970

This restaurant is a Power Lunch unto itself. The movers and shakers of Detroit do their deals here.

The food is American and Hearty. Drinks are the same.

Atmosphere is in the traditional "Club" vein, with oil paintings, leather chairs, and Toby mugs.

Service persons know why you are here, and will take your instructions to heart.

Most everything is cooked to order, including the baby back ribs, which can blow a Power Lunch to hell.

Reservations a must, unless you're known to the owner.

Expensive.

London Chop House
155 W. Congress
313/962-0278

This is a clubby, celebrity hang-out, owned by Lester Gruber, who also owns the Caucus Club across the street.

The huge oak bar dominates the lounge.

Primary emphasis is placed on comfort, from the leather banquettes to the fine tables.

Service is almost too swift and efficient. Serving persons will slow down if properly informed beforehand.

Loud to a degree, it's still a good place to see and be seen, and conduct a well planned Power Lunch.

American menu with Continental overtones.

Expensive.

Excalibur
28875 Franklin Road
Southfield
313/358-3355

If your business guest won't be distracted by the long slit in the waitress' black skirt, this restaurant offers a good opportunity for a Power Lunch in this part of the Detroit/ Southfield area.

Large booths, lots of green plants, and plenty of verbal privacy make a Power Lunch place. Many local businessmen.

Food is primarily American, with Continental inclusions. Give your waitress to understand beforehand that her recitation of the day's specials (some quite good) be given only at your direction.

Attentive service, good food, room to talk, comfortable seating.

Moderately expensive.

Van Dyke Place
649 Van Dyke
313/821-2620

Set in a 1912 French Townhouse, this classic restaurant exudes warmth and charm.

Management will permit no group larger than six persons in keeping with their desire to avoid commercialism.

Your commercialism, however, may be exercised by informing your serving persons exactly how you wish to be serviced.

Cuisine is French, expertly prepared and served. You and your guest may move from the dining room (there are three) to the drawing room to enjoy your after dinner coffee and Power Lunch conversation.

Reservations mandatory.

Expensive.

Joe Muer's Restaurant
2000 Gratiot Ave.
313/567-1088

Half a century old, and going strong.

Seafood is the excellent specialty, and is some of the best in the country.

Muer's features beamed ceilings, brick, wood and stained glass. All is immaculate, with no cute life preservers or fishnets.

Service is attentive and professional, without being annoying. A large restaurant; should make early arrangements with the Maitre d' to get a relatively quiet table location when you make your reservation.

You won't be the only business persons there.

Expensive.

SAN FRANCISCO

Vanessi's
498 Broadway
415/421-0890

Essentially three dining areas: Counter seating with a view of the kitchen; small booths located in the front of the restaurant; and, most preferable for a power lunch, the rear dining room, with comfortable banquette seating.

Large, wide ranging menu, with many Italian dishes; American dishes such as pot roast, steaks, and turkey; and peculiarly California fare such as "Hangtown fries".

Most easygoing of San Francisco suggestions.

Prices range from moderate to quite expensive.

Donatello's
In Pacific Plaza Hotel
601 Post St.
415/441-7182

Good if you are entertaining continental guests, ladies, or the very sophisticated.

Traditional and nouvelle Italian menu. Two small but equally exquisite rooms.

Good for groups of less than four, but be careful of banquette seating.

Attentive service from an exclusive staff eager to help in power lunches.

Expensive.

The French Room
In the Clift Hotel
Geary and Taylor

Serves good business breakfast as well as lunch.

Ornate, high-ceilinged, civilized room with large appointments and comfortable seating. Plenty of privacy between tables.

Masculine, no-nonsense menu of meat and seafood.

Highly professional service.

Reservations and arrangements with maitre d' recommended.

Expensive.

Sam's Grill
374 Bush St.
415/421-0594

A basic, no-frills restaurant — small, stark, and very clublike — with excellent seafood.

Highly efficient black-tied waiters serve on starched white tablecloths. No interference with business.

An institution in San Francisco, Sam's epitomizes the serious power lunch restaurant.

Reservations are not normally taken except from regulars — or strangers who make advance arrangements — who all have their own tables.

Moderately expensive.

Jack's
615 Sacramento
415/986-9854

An exact replica of the original 1860s establishment, destroyed in 1906 by the earthquake, this is a strictly masculine, no-frills restaurant.

Good lighting, high ceilings, white walls and tablecloths, wooden chairs, and a location in the financial district make Jack's the ideal setting for San Francisco power lunchers.

Varied menu includes fresh seafood and stews, as well as more unusual fare such as Jack's English mutton chop.

Ample, comfortable seating with plenty of tables and private rooms with separate entrances.

Reservations taken. No credit cards.

Moderately expensive.

Power or Wimp?

Answers to the Great American Power Lunch Test

18

Anchovies	P	Blueberry muffins	W
Apple pie	W	Blueberry pie	W
Apple pie with sharp cheddar	P	Bourbon, rocks or neat	P
Applesauce	W	Broccoli	P
Artichokes	P	Brook trout	P
Artichoke leaves	W	Brussel sprouts	P
Fresh asparagus	P	Butt steak	P
Aspics	W	Cabbage	P
Avocado	W	Calamari	P
Bacon	W	Calves liver	P
Banana Bread	W	Cantalope	W
Beef Bourgenion	P	Capers	P
Beef Oskar	W	Casseroles	W
Beef Stew	P	Cassoulet	P
Beef Stroganoff	W	Catfish	P
Beef Wellington	W	Beluga Caviar	P
Black bean soup	P	Caviar and vodka	P
Bloody Mary	P	Celery root	P
Blueberries	W	Chateaubriand	W

Cheeses:	
American	W
Bel Paese	P
Bleu	P
Brie	P
Camembert	P
Edam	W
Feta or other Greek	P
Goat Cheese	P
Gouda	W
Gruyere	P
Limburger	P
Mozzarella	W
Muenster	W
Roquefort	P
Stilton	P
Chicken ala king	W
Chicken Kiev	W
Chicken livers	P
Chicken paprikash	W
Chicken pot pie	W
Fried chicken	W
Chiffon pie	W
Chili	P
Hot Chocolate	W
Chocolate Cake	W
Chocolate Mousse	W
Cioppino	P
Clam or fish chowder	P
Steamed clams	P
Stuffed clams	P

Club soda	P
Coffee cake	W
Coke	W
Cole slaw	W
Any combination platter	W
Conch	P
Coquille St. Jacques	W
Cous-cous	P
Corned beef	W
Corned beef hash	P
Cornish hen	W
Crab legs	W
Crab Louis	W
Soft shell crabs	P
Crepes	W
Crepes Suzette	W
Daquiri	W
Date nut bread	W
Duck (half)	W
Duck — rare sliced breast	P
Eggs Benedict	W
Stuffed eggs	W
Eggplant	P
English mixed grill	P
Espresso	P
Filet	W
Fish & chips	W
Flambe "anything"	W
Flan	W
Fondues (any)	W
French fries	W

220

French onion soup	W	Lettuce Wedge	P
Fresh fruit and brie	P	Lillet	W
Frog legs	W	Lima beans	P
Fruit compote	W	Long Island iced tea	W
Fruit based mixed drinks	W	Lobster (half or whole)	P
Gin, rocks or neat	P	Lobster bisque	P
Goose liver pate	P	Lobster Newberg	W
Grilled breast of goose	P	Lobster tails	W
Grapefruit	W	London broil	P
Guacamole	W	Manhattan	P
Baked ham	W	Margarita	W
Country smoked ham	P	Marinated sliced fruit	W
Hamburger steak	P	Martini	P
Hasenpfeffer	P	Mahi mahi	W
Hearts of palm	P	Meat loaf	W
Herring	P	Melon balls	W
Horseradish dressing	P	Minnestrone	P
Hushpuppies	W	Muffins	W
Ice Cream	W	Wild mushrooms	P
Iced sherbet	W	Mussels	P
Irish Whiskey, rocks or neat	P	Noodles & cheese	W
Kidney beans	W	Omelette	W
Kiwi fruit	W	Onion rings	W
Lamb curry	P	Osso Bucco	P
Rack of lamb	W	Baked oysters	P
Rack of lamb en croute	W	Fresh oysters and clams	P
Rare lamb chops	P	Fried oysters and clams	W
Lasagna	W	Oyster mousse	W
		Paella	P
		Pancakes	W

Parfait	W	Salad bar	W
Pasta with sauce	W	Salads:	
Pears	P	Caesar salad	P
Pecan Pie	W	Carrot salad	W
Roasted peppers and anchovies	P	Chef salad	W
		Fruit salad	W
Perch	W	Greek salad	P
Perrier	W	Green salad with chunk roquefort	P
Pheasant	W		
Pickles	W	Hollywood salad	W
Pineapple	W	Hot spinach	P
Polenta	P	Salad Nicoise	W
Pork chops	W	Sliced tomato and onion salad	P
Pork shank	P		
Pork tenderloin	P	Waldorf salad	W
Stuffed pork chops	W	Salami	W
Potatoes:		Finger sandwiches	W
Baked	P	Sanka	W
Boiled	P	Sauerkraut	W
Cottage fried	P	Any sausage	W
French fried	W	Scotch, rocks or neat	P
Mashed	W	Seafood:	
Souffle	W	Salmon en croute	W
Pot roast	W	Salmon steak	P
Prime rib	W	Smoked salmon (no bagel)	P
Prime rib, bone in	P		
Prosciutto and goat cheese	P	Scottish smoked salmon	P
Quiche	W	Salt broiled sea bass	P
Ratatouille	P		
Rhubarb	P	Sashimi	P
Rice pudding	W	Scallops	W
Wild rice	P	Japanese raw scallops	P

Broiled scrod	P	Steaks:	
Seafood crepes	W	Sirloin — rare	P
Seafood gumbo	P	Roquefort sirloin	P
Shellfish cocktail	W	Sirloin with whole peppercorns	P
Shrimp cocktail	W		
Shrimp gumbo	P	Steak Diane	W
Shrimp de jonghe	W	Steak and eggs	P
Dover sole	P	Steak and kidney pie	P
Filet of sole	P	Steak tartare	P
French fried squid	P	T-bone — rare	P
Stuffed sea bass	P	Filet	W
Sushi	P	Stewed tomatoes and okra	P
Swordfish	P		
Filet of turbot	P	Strawberries	W
Whitefish	P	Strawberry shortcake	W
7-Up	W		
Shish-ke-bob	W	Stuffed tomato or avocado	W
Smorgasboard	W	Succotash	W
Souffles	W	Sweetbreads	P
Soups:		Swiss steak	W
Baked onion soup	W	Tab	W
Lentil soup	P	Tea	P
Pea soup	P	Iced Tea	W
Thin soups	W	Broiled tomatoes	P
Sour cream	P	Roast tongue	P
Sourdough bread	P	Tournedos	W
Spaghetti	W	Tuna Salad	W
Spare ribs	W	Turkey	W
Spinach	P	Braised veal shank	P
Squab	W	Broiled veal chop	W
Squash	P	Medallion of veal	P

Veal kidneys	P	Vodka, rocks or neat	P
Veal scallopini	W	Waffles	W
Mixed vegetables	W	Watercress	W
Vegetable terrine in aspic	W	Welsh rarebit	W
Vegetarian plate	W	Whiskey sour	W
Venison	P	White bread	W
Vichyssoise	P	Zabaglione	W
		Zucchini	W

"Isn't it grand, Revson? Life being just one lavish business lunch after another?"